PREVIEWS

TO BIGOTRY, NO SANCTION

NO SANCTION

Mose Durst, Ph. D.

Reverend Sun Myung Moon
and the
Unification Church

REGNERY GATEWAY • CHICAGO

Published by Regnery Gateway, Inc.
360 West Superior Street
Chicago, Illinois 60610

Distributed to the book trade by
Independent Publishers Group
One Pleasant Avenue
Port Washington, New York 11050

Manufactured in the United States of America

Library of Congress Cataloging in Publication Data
Durst, Mose, 1939-
    To bigotry, no sanction.

    Includes bibliographical references.
    1. Unification Church—Apologetic works. 2. Moon, Sun Myung. 3.
Durst, Mose 1939-   . I. Title.
BX9750.S4D88   1984   289.9   84-60571
ISBN 0-89526-609-1
ISBN 0-89526-829-9 (pbk.)

For The Reverend and Mrs. Sun Myung Moon

CONTENTS

"If anyone can show me, and prove to me, that I am wrong in thought or deed, I will gladly change. I seek the truth, which never yet hurt anybody. It is only persistence in self-delusion and ignorance which does harm."

—Marcus Aurelius

Preface

The purpose of this book is simple: to help clear up many of the confusions, misunderstandings, and false ideas about the Unification Church and its founder, the Reverend Sun Myung Moon. All major religious movements have at their inception been either misunderstood or vilified, particularly when they are transplanted to foreign soil. Although the Unification Church is rooted in the ancient traditions of Judaism and Christianity, it expresses itself through a Korean founder, and has already made a profound impact on Western culture.

There is no more controversial religious movement in the world than the Unification movement. On the one hand, the media talk about mindless "Moonies," on the other they praise shrewd "Unificationists" who established the prominent *Washington Times*. Sensationalistic articles about the church breaking up families appear in tabloid newspapers, while scholarly articles by well-respected theologians and sociologists talk about the hope for the family brought by the Unifica-

9

tion movement. In the hate-literature of anti-Unifica-
tionists, Reverend Moon is depicted as the ultimate
Svengali. In the sober assessment of many others he is a
genius who is ushering in the most significant spiritual
revolution of the twentieth century.

My experience is that ignorance underlies much
prejudice and, with respect to the Unification Church,
the public is almost completely ignorant of the simplest
of facts. I have endeavored, then, in this short book to
bare myself and my knowledge about the Unification
Church and Reverend Moon. I have not sought to
write a profound spiritual autobiography. I have attempted to provide basic information about a movement that I believe to be the most noble I have ever
encountered, and yet the most misunderstood.

The following poem, written by the cultural director
of the Korean Unification Church, epitomizes for me
the heart of Unification Church members.

Mose Durst, Ph.D.
March, 1984
New York City

THE WAY OF THE PIONEER
by Kwang Yol Yoo

Still
The non-believers are to the believers
As a vast sea to a tiny hill.
A time of heartache.

Extraordinary
Far too extraordinary tidings come over the
mountain peak.
You believe not because it's believable
But because you have to believe and want to be-
lieve.
You believe while going forward, just as I.

No matter what they say,
We,
Destined pioneers,
Go forward with faith.
First, along the confused and busy road,
One individual may fall,
His breath stop along the way,
But the whole has as much grandeur as hardship
And our confidence goes far beyond the disbelief
of others.

Brothers!
You are as valuable as your youth.
No! of more inestimable value than one can count.
Precious, beautiful, powerful jewels of heaven.

In your mind and body
Lies the fundamental ideal,
The original desire,
And love, life, and joy are blending together.

11

TO BIGOTRY, NO SANCTION

Ah!
You are blessed, chosen from the people of the
   whole world.
You are the ones who will ease God's ancient grief,
You will bring man's life to bloom.

You will put the seal of eternity on the happiness of
   home,
And you will color heaven and earth with the primary color of love,
Showing that "All people are true brothers."

Now the boat is leaving with its whistle piercing
   the air.
The promise of inevitable fulfillment
Draws near to us as time passes.

Blessed youth!
Fulfilling your mission with responsibility,
Fill the earth
With as many tents of heaven as there are people.

Let all things in the cosmos
Make haste
To reach the eternal blessed land flowing with milk
   and honey
Restoring Golgotha;
Never again will we see sin or feel pain in our con-
   sciences.
The soul will only breathe happiness
And live forever and evermore.

1 / Thou Hast Made Us For Thyself: The Background of My Quest for Meaning

"I was glad when they said unto me, let us go into the house of the Lord."

—Psalm 122

My grandmother, who lived in my parents' home until she was past a hundred years old, often repeated something similar to that passage from Psalms as she and I walked through the streets of Brooklyn on our way to the synagogue. I, for my part, was glad to walk with her. I was glad to be of some service to her, and also just to walk. Walking is a lifelong passion of mine. It is one of the earliest experiences that gave me a sense of the world and the greatness of the things God made.

Perhaps the most sincere religious feeling for me came when I lighted the Sabbath candles for my grandmother each Friday evening at sundown. She would place the white candles in the four old bronze candle holders on her bureau, the only objects in our home that seemed to me to signify permanence. My grandmother would take from her closet a prayer book that seemed not only ancient but a symbol of the mystery of our religion. She would then stand before the candles and pray. This is among the most peaceful of my childhood memories, and I loved my grandmother for her simple faith. Through her I learned to revere my elders and those whose lives were endowed with spiritual power.

I was surprised, later, to learn that my mother was uncertain about whether my grandmother was her real mother. Perhaps that uncertainty is typical of the plight of the Jew in America, who so often asks the question, "Who is a Jew?" Jews are, after all, a people who have always suffered persecution, a people who were devastated by Hitler's holocaust. As a young man, during college vacation, I walked the streets of Europe, from synagogue to synagogue, in search of my roots. Perhaps I felt a fundamental uncertainty about the meaning of my religion and indeed about the meaning of life.

Yet, if there has historically been little worldly security for the Jewish people, there has been one great spiritual security—that of the Covenant with God. And on Sabbath morning, as my grandmother and I walked to synagogue to recite the traditional prayers together with our community, we were reaffirming our trust in that basic security.

The synagogue on South Second Street in the Williamsburg section of Brooklyn was a place of mystery and of some fear for me. We would walk up the steps and enter through the huge wooden doors. I would continue to help my grandmother up to the balcony where the women sat separated from the men below. The men were praying in Hebrew, with prayer shawls wrapped in disarray around their shoulders. They were swaying back and forth while bending the knee to the mysterious God.

The greatest joy, without doubt, was walking to and from the synagogue. My grandmother would greet her friends, some too old to walk to synagogue, who sat in straightback wooden chairs against the red brick tenement buildings. Some of these same women would visit her in our kitchen after the services, and they would speak in Yiddish while helping my mother cook dinner.

My mother was like a little girl around my grandmother, and there was kitchen communion for them in the rolling of the dough and the baking of yeast cake. My father, who came to the United States from Lvov, Russia, shortly after the First World War, respected the central position of my grandmother in our household, but did not join us in our walk to synagogue. When he was a child in Europe his town was frequently bombarded, and he developed a fundamental mistrust for God, although he found within himself a kindness and compassion that he was to share abundantly with his family.

My name is Mose Durst. I was named Martin Durst at birth, but on entering the Unification Church in 1972, I took the name Mose to show my identification with the Moses of the Bible, who sought to answer God's call and do His will. I was born in Brooklyn and reared in an area inhabited by Orthodox Jews. My father, a man kept from college by the necessity of earning his own living after he emigrated from Eastern Europe, was a contractor. We were neither wealthy nor poor. I came as the third and last son at a time when my family was doing well. Immediately marked as the son to become the scholar, I was not to dirty my hands. Education was laid out before me as my portion and inheritance. Mine was a good life and my parents good parents; I did not complain then nor do I now. Nonetheless, I did feel somewhat uncomfortable over this favored treatment. In later years, when it was simply expected that I would study for law or business, I found that my heart was not in it. I tried to complete a degree that would qualify me for business, but my experiences of working in the summers convinced me that commerce was not my interest. There is really nothing wrong with commerce and business, but it was not for me. For that reason, I stayed six months longer than necessary to obtain a degree at Queens College of New York and complete an English major. It is literature, words and ideas, that are my passion. That has always been true.

I developed such a fascination while walking the streets of New York. Through walking, I encountered the city's great bookstores, and I can identify, after all these years, those that specialize in one field or another. The doorways that led to books were more exciting to me than doorways that led anywhere else.

Browsing through thousands of books, I became entranced with words and, more than with the language alone, I became enchanted with the spirit, the emotion, the heart behind the words. For me, this was the supreme experience—to be in touch with the feelings, aspirations, fears, and desires of people whom I had never known. Through books, then, I reached out and touched the heart of the humanity streaming and suffering and struggling around me.

I remember as a child how my mother would read aloud to my father, my brothers, and myself the stories of Sholem Aleichem in Yiddish, and the novels of Mark Twain in English. My mother read with a passion and delight that gave each word color, weight, texture. All of us would be moved by the joy and suffering of Jews in Eastern Europe, and by the picaresque adventures of boys in Missouri. From these stories I came to understand the life of the heart.

But walking taught me as much as books. I could not help seeing people arguing, fighting, taunting, and cursing whenever I walked. I became aware of the names we call each other, the names of intolerance and hate that echo throughout the world: Yid, Kike, Spic, Spade, Nigger, Wop. Not everyone is sensitive at heart; not everyone loves and forgives. Everywhere, people referred to others even slightly different from themselves in deprecatory terms. Yet the streets were full of all kinds of people. New York is a polyglot city, a Babel of nations, races, and faiths. On Sundays, as I walked along, there were Catholics, Lutherans, Presbyterians, Methodists, and Baptists on the way to church. There were Jehovah's Witnesses, Christian Scientists, and followers of Father Divine. Hundreds of different expressions of one basic faith in God. They moved along to temple, synagogue, cathedral, church, chapel, mission, fellowship, and prayer house. There are millions of people in the Great City and thousands of ways in which they worship God—the God to whom they look for security, but whom some forget when all appears to be going well. I became aware early on of the multitude of responses of men and women to the sheer fact of being alive. For many, living is taken for granted. Yet those countless temples testified to me that for many there is a deep desire to worship God. Something—the spirit, perhaps—moves us to praise and thank and honor and sing and worship. Oh, that we could so praise ourselves and honor our neighbor who praises in a different way! Not long ago, I took a piece of the morning's mail from my desk and looked at the commemorative stamp on the envelope. There was a picture of a fine old synagogue and a quote from George Washington: "To Bigotry, No Sanction." What a wonderful motto! Even though this is a wonderful country that ostensibly is against bigotry, there are those among us who would promote bigotry and hatred.

I learned to love this country as a young man. No one appreciates this country more than the immigrants and sons and daughters of immigrants, and New York is full of immigrants and their descendants. "To Bigotry, No Sanction." What a wonderful promise, but a vow we have not always kept in the United States. Ask the Mormons about their early history. Ask the initiates of Krishna Consciousness in West Virginia. We have not always kept our vow of tolerance when it comes to those who have new ways of praising, thanking, and knowing the God who gives us life. We have particularly not kept the vow when it comes to those who practice what social scientists call the "New Religions." The media, with unquenchable thirst for news, have named these new religions "cults," in a negative sense, and the sobriquet has stuck and is now used with a pejorative and condemnatory implication.

Although I was born a Jew, I now follow the teachings of Reverend Sun Myung Moon. I am a member of the Unification Church and, currently, its president in

America. The news media call me a "Moonie," yet I do not think of myself or my colleagues in faith as "cultists." To the contrary, in the Unification Church I know noble people who are striving to ease the suffering heart of God and to give love to the world.

I was not always a Unificationist. That title, which I take as an honor, I have held for only twelve years. Reared in the great city of New York, initiated into its many mysteries, its beauties, its challenges, and its threats, I received not only my early nourishment, but my education there as well. I did well in school. When I graduated from Queens College, I found myself eligible for a National Defense Education Act scholarship for graduate school. I debated staying in New York, which has many fine schools, but something pulled me away. Perhaps it was an unconscious desire to escape the too close security of my family. Perhaps it was a desire to see whether I could stand on my own feet. With my family, I felt overly protected. Feeling that I was given too much, and that life was not hard enough for me, I elected to go elsewhere for study.

Prior to graduate school though, I made a trip to Europe. For the first time I was alone and unsupported in a foreign land. I recall arriving in Copenhagen in broad daylight, in what would have been the middle of the night at home. Though fatigued from the long flight, I felt wide awake by the sights and sounds of a foreign city. As I walked through that beautiful Danish capital, I loved its quaintness, marked by the towering steeples of Lutheran churches, one of which had around its steeple an outside stairway twisting to the very top. How I reveled in that city, where one fre-

quently passed toyshop windows filled with lead soldiers and tiny ballerina dolls reminiscent of fairy tales
and operas. This was the exquisite land of Tivoli, a
place of peace where every opinion is allowed to flour-
ish, where one can ride boats down grand canals and
pass the statue of the Little Mermaid. This was also a
land whose Jews were spirited away and protected
when the Nazi overlords came to take them to extermi-
nation camps. What an introduction to foreign lands to
go to the fair Kingdom of Denmark!

From there I began traveling through many other
European cities, moving from place to place, always
heading south. Everywhere I searched out synagogues,
to see the remains of my ancestral people, to see what
was left after six million fellow-believers were cast into
the ovens by Nazi madmen, their ashes scattered to the
winds. What a sobering reflection! How tragic to remember the end to which bigotry can finally lead, to
walk through beautiful streets, through the imposing
cities of Europe, and to recall the pogroms and persecu-
tions that fell upon the Jews.

Walking in Frankfurt, Germany, I saw the remains
of bombed buildings. A church with one wall standing
amidst the rubble made me realize that millions who
were not Jews had also suffered terribly from the insan-
ity of war. Isolated from my family and home, I began
to feel and think in new ways. My world was no longer
New York City, and my family was becoming more
than those who lived in my home.

"Sad, that ruined building, but let me show you
some of the more beautiful sights in Frankfurt." An
American GI had approached me while I was gawking

at the church wall. I responded warmly to the friendly voice, for I always felt comforted by the presence of Americans. Unfortunately the GI on giving me the tour of Frankfurt also cleaned out my pockets. After stealing almost one hundred dollars from me he later called my hotel and attempted to coerce me into giving him even more. I left the city quickly, with less money and a little less innocence.

Upon returning from Europe, it was time to take up graduate studies. Still perplexed over where to go, I thought, with the reasoning of a youth seeking independence, that I should go as far from home as possible and still remain in the United States. So I decided to study in Oregon. There my life underwent a radical shift.

The sun was shining on the glorious bulk of Mt. Hood as I got off the plane in Portland. Portland is a beautiful town, and I fell in love with its sights and smells. After my first night there, I awoke early for my usual exploratory walk around the city. I had been walking for about thirty minutes when I came upon the synagogue in downtown Portland. Entering, I found exactly nine men; only one was lacking to form the quorum for prayer. Thus, I was greeted with warmth, duly outfitted with skullcap and prayer book, and the prayer began. Surely my journey to Oregon was being sanctified.

I experienced in Oregon, however, a very conscious identity crisis about what it meant to be a Jew. Eugene, the home of the University of Oregon, was a place with few Jews. I felt it was time for me to find out what my religion was all about, so I attended synagogue regularly. Although I was not at first aware of it, I also was looking for someone to love. I found both my Jewishness and first wife at the Eugene synagogue. When I say I found my "Jewishness" in Oregon, I mean I became acutely aware of the Jewish cultural heritage that was so much a part of my childhood environment in New York. The commitment to "menschlichkeit," to humanness, to compassion, and ethics, awakened me to a fierce pride. I was still uneasy about my religion because I did not understand my relationship to God. I found that I valued Jewish humor, Jewish literature, and Jewish food more than the Jew's covenant with God. I found I could peel off my layers of Jewish acculturation, but that I could not find a core that was the God of peace or the God of love. I was disquieted by the lack of a personal relationship with God. As I looked at those closest to me who considered themselves Jews, I found only a mirror image of myself.

Bob, a fellow graduate student at the University of Oregon, who led Sabbath services at the synagogue, was an Oregonian who adhered to the Orthodox tradition, difficult as this was in the small town of Eugene. It was friendship with him that brought me to the synagogue. I shared with him my love for Jewish humor and food, but I found in him an insecure, formalistic adherence to ritual. He resisted the intimacy of our relationship, and I found that I could not share my deep feelings with him. Years later, when I became a member of the Unification Church, he refused to see me, talk to me, or answer my letters. Apparently, he felt something deeply, although he still could not communicate to me other than through the means of silence.

On Friday nights at seven o'clock we would arrive at a darkened synagogue on the outskirts of Eugene. When Bob and I entered, he would turn on the lights in the main chapel. Slowly, cars would pull up to the building, and one by one local businessmen would enter. Sometimes a university professor would attend services, but not very often. Only one or two students would attend regularly. There would be some perfunctory greetings, then Bob would begin with the chant: "Shema, Yisroel, Adonai Elohenu, Adonai Ehud." (Here, O Israel, the Lord, our God, is One.) A brief responsive prayer with the cantor and audience would continue the service until it concluded some forty minutes later. There was a sharing of cake and coffee, then everyone would disperse. I was comforted by the coming together of community. I felt security in the chants of ancient melodies, and I was pleased to be with men who were old enough to be grandfathers. But everything was over too quickly.

I sought desperately to find meaning in my Jewishness, so I was overjoyed when at a Sabbath service I met a young Jewish girl from the university. I so hungered for someone of my own culture who could share the same touchstones of Judaism that I fell quickly in love. Several months later, after I received my Master's degree, we were married. Marriage, however, contrary to my expectations, did not clarify the meaning of my faith. Even with the two of us now attending the Friday night service, there was still a great emptiness in my heart.

I turned from the synagogue back to the library in search of life's meaning. In literature I discovered more profoundly the suffering of life as well as the triumph over that suffering through art. I could identify with James Joyce in his rebellion against the empty formalism of his church and in his devotion to art. I could sympathize with James Baldwin who understood that art must tell the tale of how we suffer, how we endure, and how we must prevail. I could "howl" with Allen Ginsberg about the madness of modern civilization, about the lack of community, and yet with him I could feel the comfort of the melodious poetic line.

Art could please and teach, but there was still the need to act if life were to be whole. I became involved in social protest. When I learned that the City of Eugene was about to cut down half its magnificent Douglas fir trees to widen several city streets, I was shocked. I had fallen in love with those trees when I came to Eugene; they were sacred to me. I organized petitions to "Save the Trees." I marched, argued at City Hall, and organized protest groups, but to no avail. The trees were cut.

I learned, however, through the experience of protest, that my love for the trees and for the city was genuine. I had suffered for what I loved. The love of nature and life, as celebrated for example in the poetry of Walt Whitman, demanded not only aesthetic response but moral action.

In the 1963-64 academic year I had the opportunity to spend the third year of my fellowship at Cambridge University in England, and it was there that I had time to reflect upon America. Although my fellowship was in medieval literature, I constantly read about the history, culture, and literature of the United States. I felt responsible to search out the traditions that were vital to American culture. I discovered the moral vision of Hawthorne and the vital language of William Carlos Williams. The beauty of art that could inform the moral sensibility became the central preoccupation of my studies.

When I returned to Oregon I began teaching, I completed my doctoral work in modern American literature, and I became painfully aware of the war in Vietnam. I now furiously organized teach-ins, protests, and fasts to alert everyone to what I perceived as the injustice of American involvement in Vietnam. The literature of protest and that of the absurd came to dominate my sensibility. My aesthetic judgments became blunted while my moral sensibility became outraged.

It was now time to establish myself as a professor. On a trip to the Modern Language Association's annual meeting, I was excited to be recruited by Lycoming College in Williamsport, Pennsylvania. The recruiters wanted to start a renaissance at the small Methodist college and were hiring thirty young, new professors to do it. I flew out to Pennsylvania and fell in love with the farseeing dean and the Lycoming Plan. I accepted the job, still looking for a place to serve.

At Lycoming, I was the typical radical young professor of the '60s. I was on the side of every cause: for protection of the environment, for civil rights, against the .growing war in Vietnam. Students regularly came to my house, where we engaged in Socratic dialogue. Then one day the progressive dean at Lycoming was fired and nearly all of the thirty new professors, including myself, immediately resigned. The professors and students at Lycoming had offered me the hope of a beautiful community as an extension of a loving family. Now, this dream was to be shattered.

At this very same time, my own marriage fell apart. Having a traditional family background, I could not even imagine divorce and I was stunned. I was especially concerned about our children. I loved them from the moment they existed as a thought and possibility, and I was deeply devoted to them. Until this day, they are the great joy of my life.

The professors and students at Lycoming had offered me the hope of a beautiful community as an extension of a loving family. Now, too, this dream was to be shattered. Community, like family, I realized, was necessary, but would not come easily. I know now that family, community, and the pursuit of an ideal were the most important things in my life, but at the time I was still not sure how to pursue all three at once.

I still did not know what to do, when a friend phoned from Oakland, California, and invited me there. As a radical, I was delighted. I moved to Oakland and began to teach at an inner-city college attended by poor Hispanics and blacks. All I could do was try to give my students basic language skills, but I saw it as my mission. I also started walking again. I arranged my schedule so that I could leave campus and walk in the countryside for hours. I began meditating; for the first time I confronted the reality of my inevitable death. I know, now, that I was searching for God.

I had come a long way, in miles and experience, since my youth in New York City. I was standing on spiritual tiptoe. I was reading spiritual classics while dipping into the new religions and psychologies that were being born in California. Actually, God was preparing me for something greater. I was to meet someone who would show me the heart of God and how I could serve Him. Her name was Onni.

2 / And Restless Are Our Hearts: Conversion to the Spiritual Community

Just as St. Augustine in middle age could look back over his life and see how God had sought him, as his restless quest for truth drove him from Manicheanism to Neo-Platonism, so I can now look back and see how the Hound of Heaven pursued me in school, teaching, and marriage. With Plato, I recognize that learning to love earthly things, coming to recognize the value of one beautiful person, is a stage on the way to loving God. One Unification theme, "tears for each other," became real for me when I met Onni, the hardworking, fully dedicated missionary who later became my wife.

The story of my conversion may be unremarkable, although it moved me deeply and still does. I reluctantly record how the Spirit dealt with me, only because my experience demonstrates conclusively the deep spirituality of the Unification movement. There is no place for the misunderstanding and prejudice of "brainwashing" charges, of declarations that "Moonies" hold people against their will or exploit them, when we see the process by which individuals identify with the movement.

I came to Oakland, a disappointed but by no means

broken man. The work with poor youth was demanding but satisfied my deep desire to serve others. I helped establish, among other projects, the interdisciplinary program at Laney College. I began reading spiritual classics of East and West, analyzing, on this American frontier closest to the Orient, the contributions of the East to human spiritual development.

Later I was to learn that a basic Unification ideal is the incorporation of the sacred in the secular world: a move to make concrete the holy, the loving, and the good in the midst of parking lots, classrooms, and streets of the real, selfish world. I can see now that this basic religious ideal was what attracted me when I first became aware that *someone* was different from all the other people I had previously met.

One needs to remember that there was no Unification Church, as such, in the United States in 1971 when I first became aware of a new teaching in Oakland. There was a Unification Church corporation, a formal entity, but only a handful of members in the San Francisco Bay area, in Los Angeles, in Washington, and in New York. Someone familiar with my interdisciplinary studies course told me of a Korean woman who lived on Dana Street, in Oakland, who might have some interesting ideas to share. Fresh from an improvisational dance class—I was involved in *many* consciousness raising activities—I went to 6502 Dana Street and rang the bell. A lovely Korean woman invited me in.

The apartment was small but immaculately clean. Bright California sunlight streamed through the orange and white curtains onto the blue felt sofa where she invited me to sit. I was later to find, to my amusement and surprise, that to save money several dresses and ties worn by members of the church were made of exactly the same material as the curtains. Onni sat on the couch and wore a long, modest woollen dress. I do not believe I ever saw her legs until about a year later, when she arrived at the San Francisco airport wearing a dress Mrs. Moon had given her.

What immediately struck me about her was her smile. She seemed so normal and happy, quite at ease with herself, yet open and responsive to the stranger who sat down in her living room. She had dark brown hair, brown eyes, and was a soft presence in a warm room. We spoke briefly, but she was quick to ask me what I did and how I liked my work. Her directness was disarming, especially in contrast to her warmth. She did not speak much during our first meeting, but I was aware that she was very much the "center" of this small spiritual community.

I visited her regularly in this little apartment and she willingly talked. I was intrigued by her teaching, delighted over the charts she showed me which detailed the relationship of man to God, and fascinated by her personality. I was not familiar with Reverend Moon, whom she called her teacher, and it was hard for me to imagine what he could be like. She offered me a copy of the *Divine Principle,* Reverend Moon's central book of doctrine, which I had never seen or heard of before.

I later learned that Onni had joined the Unification Church in Japan in 1960. She was working at the Korean embassy in Tokyo at the time when she first met Mr. Sang Ik Choi, the first missionary sent by Reverend Moon to Japan from Korea in 1958. Onni was one of the first ten members of the Japanese Unification Church, and very soon after joining she became a pioneer missionary to the city of Shimonoseki. She had left her job at the embassy, and set out with great hope to communicate the central message of the Unification Church: that God suffers and longs for the love of His lost children, the human race. Shortly after I met Onni in Oakland I asked her why she came to America. "To end God's suffering," she replied, "and to end the suffering of human history."

In 1965, when the Japanese church had grown significantly, Reverend Moon sent Mr. Choi and two successful missionaries from Japan to the United States. Onni was chosen along with Mr. Kenji (Daikon) Ohnuki. They thus joined the earliest missionaries from Korea in the United States: Dr. Young Oon Kim, who came in 1959; Col. Bo Hi Pak, who came in 1961, and Mr. David S.C. Kim, who also arrived in 1959.

Pioneering in Japan and the United States, I was to learn, was filled with much walking, little food, and constant praying. I can never look at Onni's feet without thinking of the hundreds of miles she walked in seeking to communicate the message of God's suffering heart to an indifferent world. Even when she pioneered Oakland, California, she would walk around Lake Merritt several hours a day until she met someone with whom she could share God's heart and her own desire to love another human being. Her English was poor when she first came here, so she had to rely on prayer, perseverance, and a joyful smile to spread her message.

Kristina Morrison Seher joined Onni, becoming the second member of the Oakland Unification Church.

They lived together in a small, one-bedroom apartment on Telegraph Avenue near Berkeley. Kristina was pursuing her doctoral studies in psychology at the University of California, Berkeley, while working as an educational consultant. Onni, holding down two jobs as a waitress, worked a total of sixteen hours a day when she first arrived in San Francisco. She would then "witness"—share the ideas of the church—for three to four hours with anyone who would listen. With Kristina working, Onni then had the opportunity to witness many hours a day.

Onni would rise at 4:30 a.m., awaken Kristina, and then prepare for prayer at five. Then both women would study the *Bible,* the *Divine Principle,* or other sacred texts. They would set their goals for the day, eat breakfast, and set out for the day's activities. In the evening Onni would usually bring home for dinner one or two guests with whom she would share the ideals of the Unification movement.

Both Kristina and Onni are devout and powerfully motivated women. Even in our church, and certainly outside, they are held somewhat in awe because of their commitment, their dedication, and their love of God. Many times both women have fasted seven days so that America would be blessed by God, their sacrifice offered as a condition of purity so God would have mercy on the many profane actions of our nation. They have fasted for President Nixon and they have fasted so often for a brother or sister who was suffering.

The fasting, praying, and sacrificing took their toll on Onni's health. She contracted tuberculosis and was confined to her room for almost a year. I once asked her why she didn't lose faith during this period, since she had done so much for God and He seemed to do so little for her. "What do you mean little?" she replied sharply (and there certainly is a sharp as well as a soft side to Onni). "I have life, I have love, and I have my ideals. I am an earthly-down person. I can pray for my brothers and sisters, I can sing holy songs, and I can now study. I have even been given a copy of a book by Swedenborg from Dr. Young Oon Kim. No problem. No worry."

Onni loved Kristina deeply, and both women eventually brought several thousand dedicated members to the Unification Church. The secret of their success was simple: deep faith, constant prayer, sincere sacrifice for others, and joyful love of God. As I look at those people who received spiritual life from Onni, I see physicians like Dr. William Bergman, professors like Dr. Tyler Hendricks, businessmen like Jeremiah Schnee, and a myriad of others, including myself.

When I first met Onni, I was already prepared for a spiritual charge, through my practice of meditation, my wide reading in spiritual subjects, and my interdisciplinary course. Nevertheless, my conversion was not to come suddenly. I was familiar with the theories of psychologists like Abraham Maslow and Erik Erikson, and their concepts of gradual, evolving change until there is a growth of the personality and spirit. Now that spiritual evolution was to take place in me.

The self-sacrifice, humility, and basic goodness of Onni deeply impressed me. I valued modesty and self-lessness, but had been disappointed repeatedly by people I admired such as professors and teaching colleagues, who behind their facade of knowledge and service, had hidden agendas for seeking power or sex. I prized personal purity. There were of course many opportunities for promiscuous sex in California, and everywhere, in the 1960s and '70s, but I did not take advantage of them. I was repelled by such casual approaches to something as meaningful, and to me sacred, as human sexuality. The purity of Onni and the genuine absence of lust and self-seeking in the few people drawn to this new teaching made the greatest impression on me. Here were people who were real, who meant what they said. They were, precisely, not deceptive, not out for profit or the satisfaction of their own desires. I was moved. Onni once said to me, when I marvelled at her poise and giving: "We must be value-makers and happy-makers." The Unification people I met were exactly that: searchers for absolute values who tried to live those values. I found that I wanted to become like them, to give value and happiness, to make service the core of my life.

I remember coming over one evening to Dana Street after a long day of teaching. I walked in the front door of the house, which was situated next to the playground of a Catholic church in a lower-middle class neighborhood. I walked into the foyer, took my shoes off (I never knew whether this was for the sake of cleanliness or spirituality, although the action did make me feel cleaner and more spiritual), and sat on the couch. I was in an introspective mood when I chanced to look at the couch on the other side of the room. An old, crippled man was being served coffee by Jennifer Morrison while her brother Matthew was engaged with him in an animated conversation. (Kristina was able to bring to the movement her two sisters, brother, and parents.) Watching the genuine care of Jennifer and Matthew for the old man prodded me out of my moodiness.

I am often asked what people find in the Unification movement that they are unable to find in other religious communities. Well, certainly the quality of serious and genuine commitment to spiritual ideals is a central part of what moved me. Further, to experience a community of people who seek together to realize these ideals is extraordinary, uplifting, and totally nourishing. A caring creative community was what I encountered at 6502 Dana Street, and it is what I continually try to recreate whenever and wherever I am with church members.

To this day, I find one pervasive misunderstanding about Unificationists. Though we ourselves take the religious impulse to be the central impulse of life, society for the most part disbelieves that this can truly be our primary motivation. Religion may be important to many people, but it is seldom the core of their daily existence. For us, the ground upon which we stand is holy.

Professor James Fowler, in his classic study *Stages of Faith,* describes the mature human being as one who has reached the culmination of psychological and spiritual maturity:

> . . . [such a person] becomes a disciplined activist *incarnation*—a making real and tangible—of the imperatives of absolute love and justice. . . . The self [at this stage]. . . engages in spending and be-

ing spent for the transformation actuality. Persons best described by [this stage]...engage in spending and being spent for the transformation of present reality in the direction of a transcendent actuality. Persons best described by [this stage] ...typically exhibit qualities that shake our usual criteria of normalcy. The heedlessness to self-preservation and the vividness of their taste and feel for transcendent moral and religious actuality give their actions and words an extraordinary and often unpredictable quality. In their devotion to universalizing compassion they may offend our parochial perceptions of justice. In their penetration through the obsession with survival, security, and significance they threaten our measured standards of righteousness and goodness and prudence. Their enlarged visions of universal community disclose the partialness of our tribes and pseudo-species....[1]

This was the kind of happy normality I saw shining forth from Onni's face. If she ever had what might be described as "glazed eyes," it was usually after a prayer in which she had been crying for God's ancient grief and for the suffering of the world. I have come to believe that if we do not on some occasions have such glazed eyes, we have truly lost our souls.

[1] From an adaptation of *Life Maps: Conversations on the Journey of Faith* by Jim Fowler and Sam Keen, edited by Jerome Berryman, copyright © 1978 by Word Inc. as used in *Stages of Faith* by Jim Fowler Harper & Row, 1981); use by permission of Word Books, Publisher, Waco, Texas 76796.

I returned to Dana Street over and over again. I began to discuss, to ask questions, to take part. I came to see that ideals and values were meant to be made real each moment in even the smallest actions. I realized, too, the incompleteness of the classroom experience. Ideas could elicit a certain passion, and I could pour myself out for ideas I believed to be true, but there was no obligation to live those ideas. In fact, there is almost an unwritten contract in the classroom that no idea will affect anyone's immediate life too much. My conversations with Onni, however, brought me to the realization that each individual is an embodiment of God's nature, and that each person has the potential and responsibility for expressing God's love powerfully and deeply. "Our lives are to reflect the divine nature," Onni said, and I saw the divine reflected in her.

Onni's humor and down-to-earth practicality also moved me. Her laughter struck me as being singularly beautiful. Much later, I was to meet Reverend Moon and hear his laughter, too. The way of God, I realized, is joy. As I came to have a concrete and sweet vision of what my life could be like, I identified with Onni and her fledgling movement. I threw open my home for church activities. It became, in effect, a Unification Church. I moved out of my bedroom and began sleeping on the floor with other "brothers" who used my house. I gave over direction of the household to a man younger than myself, who became our elder, or leader. I was moving towards complete identification with the few dozen members of the Unification Church in California—for that was our size in 1972. I was never happier. I saw these people as good and pure, bright and normal. They were living out the spiritual ideas I had previously only talked about in my classes.

As my home became a church center, I could recognize why most religious movements began with a small group of people trying to live the ideals of a religious founder. The foundation of a religious movement depends not only on the greatness of the visionary or the vision, but on the ability of a religious community to practice the ideals and traditions of that vision. For the last ten years in the United States a broad and deep foundation for our movement has been established by dedicated, self-sacrificing people.

The church center was and is a place for the caring, loving community to actualize its ideals, not in isolation from the world, but in service to the world. There is a tremendous value to people praying, studying, and working together. Throughout history religious communities have known this. The goal of our church centers, however, has always been to wither away, so that the family and home will become the center of nourishment and support where God dwells.

The fulfillment of our church work is to reach out to entire families within a community, then to build a network of 360 families in service to God. Every member of our church is asked to minister to 360 homes within a particular community. This is true of all our churches, now in over 127 countries. It is called "Home Church." Without mature, dedicated members (called priests, ministers, or rabbis in other traditions) there can be no model for "Home Church" members. The service and ministry we offered to those in the neighborhood of my house was simple. We would pray for people, offer to do small tasks from gardening to house cleaning, and invite our neighbors to our home to share in fellowship, love, and study of our movement's teachings.

The public and media simply fail to understand that this is the way a religious movement evolves. In the United States during 1972-1983, the Unification movement grew very rapidly, members exhibiting an extraordinary degree of commitment. This intensity was seen as fanaticism rather than the necessary activity for the establishment of a religious movement. The religious impulse is all too often suspect, for it challenges us to look critically at how we are living our lives.

My growing attachment to the religious community was not just emotional. I knew, and had felt, religious emotion before, for the prayers at synagogue had stirred mixed emotions in me. I knew that emotion alone was not enough. My reason had to be challenged, too. Onni, with her lectures and charts, discussed with me the problem of evil. We talked at length about arrogance, pride, and selfishness. We analyzed the fundamental problem of the misdirection of love in the world and in our lives. People adored things they ought not to worship and did not love what they should. We looked at how this problem had existed from the beginning of history as we surveyed the historical concept of "idolatry," or "false love," in Judaism and Christianity.

Onni frequently visited the small community we established in my home. Sometimes she visited my college classes. Each morning I got up early, prayed, helped clean the house, then took my briefcase and went out to teach literature. I was moving closer to God, but He had not yet captured me. Then, in His own time, He did.

My conversion was not startling; no outward miracle took place. Just as God finally reached Augustine while he was reading the Epistles of Paul, He reached me while I was praying with my new brothers and sisters. In my own home, in the midst of a simple prayer service similar to many others in which I had engaged, I was powerfully shaken to the foundations of my being.

Onni always stressed the basic nature of sincere prayer. She tried to teach me to pray from the heart, to follow Paul's teaching that we should pray without ceasing. I was praying often and benefitting from it, but on this day there was a change from quantity to spiritual quality. Even now my whole body lights up and tingles as I think of that unforgettable, life-changing moment.

I was praying as powerfully as I could, surrounded by my friends, when I felt a sloughing off of the past, an unburdening of guilt and sadness. That prayer cleaned me out; it was catharsis in the most primal way. It was as if thousands of years of accumulated spiritual dead-weight was falling away from me. I felt clean, whole, purified, down to the center of my being. I remember thinking, *this* is what life is meant to be; this is how I want to spend the rest of my life; no, the rest of eternity! I knew, consciously, what my unconscious was feeling: that I had discovered the deepest part of myself and had discovered, and been claimed by God.

I could not keep this to myself. I shared it with my brothers and sisters who rejoiced with me. I shared with Onni, and from that moment on I knew that I would be part of this movement for the rest of my life, forever. I shared my joy even more. I telephoned my mother in New York, declaring "Mom, I have discovered God. Now I know the meaning of my existence." It was wonderful to give her such hope, for I knew that she had been searching for God her entire life. Later my parents became associate members of the church.

But this was not only an ethereal experience. Like all else Onni taught me, it was practical, pragmatic, "earthly down." I saw how I could be master of my own destiny. I knew now what I wanted out of life: I wanted deep, pure, serving, and loving relationships. I now recognized the pure from the impure. I saw who was pure and serving and who was not. I found my true spiritual guide, my Beatrice and Virgil, the earthly and the heavenly conductor, all in one. My spriritual guide, my soulmate, was Onni. The veil was lifted from my eyes.

I saw, too, that I was no pushover. I was tough and strong inside. Nothing could stop me. I had been waiting all my life to be used for some high purpose, and now I had found that purpose. Although Onni was not present at that prayer service, I saw that she was the sacramental means, the earthly instrument, who had made it possible. So I went to her to learn the source of her strength, her love, and her faith. She became my spiritual parent.

3 / The Spiritual Parent and the Spiritual Community

Onni, my spiritual parent, never had any doubt about the reality of the spiritual world. Inspired by the vision, she took on the role of spiritual parent to me by raising me up to a large vision, a great love, and a grand commitment to an idea. The spiritual childrearing began with a focus on meditation, introspection and, above all, to a life of constant prayer. As a spiritual parent she was to teach me about prayer as a way to know myself and to know God.

I remember those powerful prayers with her as well as the quiet and gentle ones, the strong prayers of exhortation and the sorrowful prayers of repentance. My first prayer with Onni took place on a Sunday morning at Lake Merritt in Oakland several weeks after I met her in 1972. Reverend Moon, on his first world tour in 1965, dedicated "holy grounds" in forty nations. These are essentially prayer grounds dedicated to God and to His purpose. Church members often go to these prayer grounds to pray to God for the world, for their nation, and for their city. They may then dedicate additional "holy grounds" in their own cities. A small grove of pine trees near Lake Merritt is the "holy ground" in Oakland.

Church members regularly go to holy grounds at five a.m. on Sunday morning. As in other religious traditions, we rise early and seek first to claim the world for God before the world has a chance to sin. On this particular Sunday, Onni wore a long quilt dress with a huge purple coat. About twelve of us arrived at the lake, scattered about the grove, and then, one by one, began to pray. My heart beat quickly as the childhood scene of the synagogue flashed back into my mind. The prayer here seemed, like the one in the synagogue, somewhat strange and a little disconcerting. I heard, however, Onni crying out to God that she might comfort His heart and that He could use her life for His purpose. I began to understand the meaning of the devoted child who seeks to comfort the grieving parent.

I myself began praying instead of listening. I felt a certain strength coming from within me. I felt a connectedness to the huge pine tree in the center of the holy ground, to the lake, to those praying around me, and to the God whom I wanted so desperately to know and feel. I felt as though I were awakening from a long sleep.

I can visualize Onni quietly praying on her knees by the small table in her room, and I can hear the powerful volume of her prayers as she stands amidst swirling fog atop Twin Peaks in San Francisco. I can see her praying in the Berkeley Hills, overlooking the lovely lights of the city. I hear the passionate prayer she offers at the end of a seminar in Boonville, California.

Prayer, then, was the primary way that Onni sought to guide me and take responsibility for my spiritual life. The basis of the parent-child relationship is trust and love centered upon a valued purpose. If we feel that our parents love us, and if we value the purpose of their lives, then we trust that they will be able to guide us properly, and we are generally willing to follow their guidance. Onni was guiding me into a knowledge of God and into an awareness of God-centered ethical action.

A parent is one who is responsible for raising a child physically, morally, and spiritually. In our own culture, however, because of the tremendous breakdown of families, children often lack or mistrust moral and spiritual guidance. Consequently, adults are often moral and spiritual infants. We frequently resent the advice of our parents because we don't respect the purpose of their lives; the very concept of parent is denigrated. Many young people no longer wish to assume the burden of parenthood.

The church and school that have historically functioned *in loco parentis* become objects that young people rebel against or view with indifference. We sometimes think of a parent as someone who controls or dominates by sheer power. It is rare that a young person trusts the wisdom and love of his parents. It is even rarer that the wisdom and love of parents can lead one to an understanding and love of God.

A spiritual parent in the Unification movement seeks to teach about God as the parent of mankind. We come to know God's parental heart by caring for and loving others. As we seek to be an example of a true parent, we care for those who are physically and spiritually younger than we are. We refer to Reverend and Mrs. Moon as the "True Parents" of our church, for we believe that they give us a God-centered wisdom and love by which we may mature in our spiritual lives. We thus hope to become "true parents" ourselves; we have this hope for all human beings.

Ironically, as we in the Unification movement seek to give God's parental love to a world that resembles an orphanage, we set ourselves up as objects of hate and rebellion. By genuinely seeking to care for others, we may act foolishly, especially if we are immature. Further, the unresolved conflicts individuals have with their physical families will be carried over to their spiritual parents. Gaining spiritual life and giving it to others, from my experience, is the most difficult process imaginable.

Tragically, some parents have reacted bitterly when church members speak of spiritual parents, or of Reverend and Mrs. Moon as "true parents." The physical parent feels threatened, and feels the child (the adult child that is, for the average age of church members in the United States is 28 years) no longer loves him. This, indeed, is tragic, for our purpose is to recreate a God-centered love within the family. Every member of our church is taught to love his family as the central unit through which God can establish His ideal on earth.

In the early years of the Unification movement in the United States, individuals have given of themselves with a great dedication that has not always been to the liking of their families. "Why don't you spend time in your hometown? Why don't you take over the family business? Why don't you spend time with us, your real family?" These concerns are genuine, and individuals must always be responsible for working out their unique situations. Nevertheless, a religious calling has always demanded hard choices.

It must have been very difficult for Abraham, father of the Jewish faith, to reconcile his religious calling with the demands of his father, the idol maker. The parents of Saint Francis were outraged by his decision to abandon a promising commercial future. How could he talk about loving his Heavenly Father and all of creation, when he didn't even listen to or love his own family? Saint Thomas Aquinas' family did not at first look favorably upon their son's religious calling. He was abducted by his mother and brother and imprisoned in a tower with a prostitute, in an effort to tempt him away from his religious commitment.

Several years ago in San Francisco I introduced a young man to our movement after he had graduated from an East Coast college. I sought to share with him whatever love and understanding I possessed. He was moved by our ideals, by our loving community, and by the purposeful direction he could give his life. Several weeks after he became involved with our church, his parents came to visit. The father was fearful about his son, hateful toward me, and mistrustful of everything going on. He had no questions to ask, of course, and feigned indifference to his son's involvement. Not long afterwards the young man was kidnapped by criminals hired by his parents. Held in an isolated setting for several weeks, he was accused incessantly of being brainwashed until finally his trust in our church was broken. Then he was immediately rushed to the media, where he could make a "true confession" about the false, deceptive love in our church, and about myself as the chief deceiver. All I could feel was a pain, as though I had been kicked in the heart.

If I felt some suffering for my spiritual son, I was made even more aware of the central reality of our spiritual life: God suffers. I was to learn that the major responsibility of life is to be a representative of God in the world. Whenever I talk to anyone, I feel I have to represent God's heart and God's love to him or her. If a person attends a seminar, comes into the church, or is just a friend, I, as the spiritual parent, try to live for that person. For if God is a being of love, of care, and of nourishment, then I can resemble God most by loving, caring, and nourishing others. The way I grow as an individual is to live for someone else. When I speak to a spiritual child, I try to do so with a purposeful heart of love. If my spiritual child has greater wisdom and love than I do, then I receive even more than I give, and I am then in the role of spiritual child. And if my spiritual child returns hatred for my love, all I can do is continue to love and remember the One who suffers for everyone's hatred.

It is not uncommon for a spiritual parent to fast three, four, even seven days in sacrifice for the well-being of his spiritual child. On my own prayer list are spiritual children who committed their lives to God over ten years ago. Spiritual parenting is not a technique. Like prayer itself, the desire to be a spiritual parent means that we must constantly extend the most sincere part of our being toward the welfare of another. Every individual is confronted with loneliness, grief, despair. If, however, we have the entire human family as a source of comfort and sustenance, then where is the evil? The immediate, *concrete* realization we have when we become a spiritual parent is that we are all connected to God, who is our Heavenly Parent. When we in the Unification movement speak of each other as brothers and sisters, this is a reality to us; it is not mere words.

On God's Day (a Unification Church Holy Day celebrated on January 1,) 1973, I wrote in my diary:

> It has been a beautiful, full, and fulfilling first day of the year. When we returned from Mendocino yesterday, then went into San Francisco for the ten p.m. God's Day ceremony, I didn't realize how rich and joyful the day would be. It is so clean and good now to dedicate my life to serve mankind. The *Divine Principle* seems so simple at the moment:
> * To think always of others first
> * To do for others first
> * To have faith in Heavenly Father, and
> * To understand that Heavenly Father wants to restore mankind.
>
> It seems obvious that I—and our spiritual family—must be an example to the world and to this country of our total dedication to others.

After joining the church, it became clear that we needed a home for spiritual parenting. That is why Boonville, our seminar facility, was begun. Boonville simply was a place to teach the *Divine Principle* to inquiring people. It was and is a classical religious retreat center. We did not use duplicity to get people to visit Boonville, and certainly *never* used force to hold them there against their will. To the contrary, so important is it to maintain a positive spiritual and educational atmosphere at a workshop that we gladly would encourage anyone to leave who did not want to stay. We did not want hostility to poison the atmosphere. The spiritual retreat at Boonville was meant to be an environment where one could study ideals and seek to actualize them in the midst of like-minded people.

Boonville, California, is a small town about 120 miles north of San Francisco. The seminar facility is actually a former sheep ranch nestled in the hills of Mendocino County, about twenty miles from the Pacific Ocean. Several house trailers were purchased and placed on the flat part of the land, below the hills, next to a creek. About forty acres of cultivated land fronts the highway, which runs through the town to the coast. An apple orchard, which yields abundant harvest, is situated on one part of the front land.

The first time I arrived in Boonville, on a Friday night, from the San Francisco Bay area, I was struck with the fresh air, bright star-filled sky, and pervasive sense of peace. I took my sleeping bag and walked over the small bridge that crossed the creek, to the large white trailer which was reserved for men. There were about fifteen brothers in the trailer, and we immediately unrolled our sleeping bags and readied for sleep after the long drive from San Francisco.

I awoke in the morning at seven a.m. to the sound of a guitar and someone singing "You are my sunshine." There was a sense of excitement as to what the day would bring. After cleaning up, I walked out of the trailer and was struck by the vividness of the green grass and blue, cloudless sky. My host for the weekend, a young man who was also a church member, was anxious to be friendly and attend to my needs, to act as my spiritual parent for the weekend.

Although to this day the pattern of a weekend seminar, or a weeklong seminar, remains essentially the same, I am always struck by how the simple environment of a country retreat allows one to contemplate the most complex questions of life. I am reminded of how Thoreau's desire, in going to Walden, was to "simplify, simplify, simplify." Once Thoreau could simplify life, he could then ponder the serious, complicated questions about the nature of God and God's work in the world.

The great power of a Unification seminar, at Boonville or anywhere else, is the theme of the lectures and discussion. How often can one set aside several days to think about God, His nature, and creation? How often do people take time, in depth, to examine their relationship with God? How often do people examine the nature of evil and the tragedy of human history? How often do people question how they can most effectively work together to actualize God's ideal in human community? These are the topics of lecture-discussions at any Unification seminar, and they were the topics at my first seminar, when my mind and heart began to awaken to a new realization of God in my life.

Many books about the Unification doctrine have now been written by scholars who are not themselves Unificationists. Professor Herbert Richardson of the University of Toronto (formerly of Harvard University) has said that the *Divine Principle* is perhaps the most significant theology of the twentieth century. But how have the media dealt with Boonville and Unification principles? By writing about the food or the alleged and non-existent barbed wire fences.

I know of almost no article, out of thousands written about us, that deals with the content of Unification teaching. News media emphasize the "indoctrination techniques" as opposed to the reality of three one-hour lectures each day followed by discussion. At times, newspapers talk of Unificationists "love-bombing" those who attend. Such a cynical description! Where else can one truly feel the love of God if not in an environment dedicated to expressing it?

Even the lovely environment of the Mendocino country has been reduced by the media to the fifty feet (total length) of deer fence that surrounds our vegetable garden. Our seven hundred acre ranch, which borders other hills and ranches, could not be adequately fenced in by the U.S. Army. Yet, endless stories appeared as to "How I Escaped from Moonie Stronghold." The bus station in the town of Boonville is five hundred yards from our ranch's entrance.

Boonville was always meant to be an environment where our spiritual community could build its foundation through caring relationships. Spiritual parenting is a large part of the dynamics of every seminar. Every church member feels that he must act as an elder, a parent, to his guests by caring for them, serving them, and teaching them. Unfortunately, this has not always been done in the most comprehensive way, for the spiritual parent has often been a young church member and the guest sometimes resents being cared for. This simple failure of relationships has sometimes led to the false charges of "pressure" and "coercion" as techniques used by the Unification Church.

I remember a wealthy lady who came to Boonville in the summer of 1974 for a weekend seminar. She was invited by a woman in her early twenties who had been a member of our church for several weeks. I noticed these two women during breakfast on Saturday morning, for the older one wanted to take a walk in the woods and the younger was anxious to explain that the purpose of the weekend was to participate in a seminar. Somehow, both women managed to arrive in the lecture hall about a half-hour late. I learned later that the guest wanted to dominate the discussion hour by explaining some facts about astrology. She was asked by our sister to focus her remarks on the content of the lecture. The lady was indignant. Finally, after dinner, everyone was asked to participate in a group song. The lady could bear the experience no longer and left in a huff, asking to be driven back to San Francisco. For many months after, we heard stories about this woman's terrible experience at Boonville.

No news article ever spoke about drug abuse, sexual exploitation, or criminal behavior at Unification seminars. There was none. The complaint, as it has more or less appeared in mental health legislation in various states, was that people who came to our seminars often changed 180 degrees. They no longer acted as they had in the past. Sacrifice, public mindedness, and public spirit were the virtues we sought to teach, and people rarely came to our seminars with an abundance of these.

Through care, respect, and love, and not by fear, hypnotism, or brainwashing, we seek to draw out the individual's divine potential. Rather than doing anything to drag a person down, we seek always to build someone up. We have always discouraged and proscribed the taking of drugs, liquor, or cigarettes, and we discourage sexual promiscuity. We exhort people to respect the body as a temple of God, and hope to inspire those who have experienced our Unification community to establish a God-centered family of their own.

When people hear our ideals they sometimes feel threatened. They've become used to boxing themselves up in little rooms and are fearful that they may have to encounter the depth of themselves and the full challenge of life. We teach that it is necessary to stand up for ideals in an age that often scorns them. We encourage the young to love their country, but, more importantly, we emphasize the need to love the world. Though we teach people that the great heroes of the world were Buddha, Moses, Jesus, we point out that every nation has its righteous men and women. We teach people how to sing and "make a joyful noise unto the Lord." We teach those in our seminars to reflect God's nature, *to imitate Christ*. That is the basis of our life. It is an ideal that is scorned by the world. It is considered crazy. Well, if the world is normal as it is, we choose to be crazy. That is the ultimate basis of our life. It is the basis of the road that Jesus walked. It is the declared basis of the Roman Catholic and Protestant churches. We are receiving the same scorn and rejection Jesus did, and we are happy to take it if it helps others become more loving and giving. That is our purpose. And that is what goes on at that "awful Boonville place"!

The seminar, of course, was never an end in itself. On Sunday night most people returned to their life in the city. At most, out of those guests who were new, perhaps ten percent would stay for a seven-day or twenty-one day seminar. But then they too would have to return to the city to deal with the complexities of a world not seeking to embody God's ideal. I had to return to teaching my classes at an inner-city college; Dr. George, another member, would return to his computer firm; Kristina would return to her consulting job.

In the early days of our movement in the United States, most single members lived in church centers. These were either small centers like the one on Dana Street, or larger ones such as the fraternity house across from campus on Hearst Street in Berkeley. This latter house, of course, was dubbed the "Hearst mansion" by the media. According to them, Unification members never live in houses, only mansions. And Reverend Moon never lives in parsonages owned by the church, only on estates.

The members' living situations were somewhat unique to the United States. In Korea and Japan, as well as in other countries, members usually live in their own apartments or houses and attend worship services or other activities in a community church center. Of course, wherever the movement sent out missionaries there would be an initial stage in which members would live in a church center while establishing a larger foundation.

Now that a strong foundation has been laid in the United States, most of our members are married, they have begun their families, and they live in their own homes and work at jobs just like members of any other faith. The goal of the Unification movement is not to build a new denominational community, but rather to strengthen the larger human community.

The value of a spiritual community, however, within a church center or within the larger community, is central to the intentions of the Unification movement. Ultimately, we see the family and home as the basic building block for God's ideal in the world. We believe the home should be where God dwells, and that a mature man and woman are the fullest reflections of His nature. We believe parents should give not only physical life to children, but spiritual life, too. The family and the community in modern society are not of the ideals God intended. The spiritual community, or spiritual family, can be the transitional element in uplifting the larger human community.

The elements guiding the daily life of Unification members are devotion, study, and service. When my wife lived by herself, as she pioneered in Oakland, she prayed at five a.m. each morning, sang holy songs after prayer and studied. In the evening she would try to visit those who she believed needed God's truth and love. Finally, she would return home and pray again before going to bed. This remains the basic pattern of a Unification Church member's life.

Prayer to God is the core of our life, and we continually receive new awareness about God and ourselves through the process of prayer. We try to train ourselves to be pure vessels that God can fill with His holy love. Prayer, moreover, is not limited to formal moments. We pray at all times and in the most unusual places. I remember my wife and I praying at a parking meter before we were to visit a friend. What a holy altar! My assistant Jeremiah and I have prayed in numerous elevators. I prayed in my office at the college before each of my classes. I prayed that God could use me as a teacher, and I prayed that I could value, respect, and love my students, even when neither I nor they were so lovable.

Members of our movement are continually filled with the spirit of God's creativity, and they have created numerous poems, songs, dances, and other works of art. Not a day or week goes by without some new creation. Reverend Moon himself has written songs like the following:

> Come, my brethen, spring has come to the Garden and the flowers bloom.
> Brethen, sing happily, sing for the spring.
> All come, dance, and sing new songs.
> Come, my brethen, into the Garden,
> The Garden of flowers where we dance to a song of joy.
> All my brothers are happy; they all gather and dance to a new song.
> Come, my brothers, gather in the Garden.
> Sing your happy song.
> My brothers of Eden with eternally glad hearts,
> All gather and dance to new songs.
> > (Translation from the Korean)

I have found that when people are motivated by high ideals, and where there is a spirit of care and cooperation that pervades a community, creativity overflows.

One of our members is now completing a major American opera about California; it will be produced this year. A graduate student who is a member of our church and who is working on his Ph.D. at Harvard, just notified me that an article of his has been published in the *Harvard Theological Review*. Several of our members who work on a New York daily newspaper have just received prizes in journalism. And I would give a prize for my sister Judyann's coffee cake.

When people in our community create, they genuinely want to bring joy to others. The purpose of life, we believe, is to experience joy, by fulfilling our God-centered love and ideals in service to others. But just because our purpose is joy does not mean that we do not experience the entire range of emotions. As I write this chapter in New York, my wife is on a church-related trip to Korea, and my beloved children are at home with my in-laws in California. This is very painful to me; I would rather our family be together each day. But I realize that the larger human family needs my work here in New York today, and it needs me at a revival meeting in Kansas tomorrow. Most of our members who are establishing the foundation for our movement in America are making similar sacrifices.

Some accuse us of working many hours a day, not caring enough for our families, and being hopelessly naive in our idealism. Well, I do not know of any member of our movement who enjoys sacrifice as a kind of sadism. We are all hurt when our loved ones do not understand the nature of our sacrifice, as we are hurt when those who do not love us do not care about our sacrifices. We are sober super-realists who understand the difficulty of trying to make the world a better place and of trying to make ourselves better people.

What is different about us is our purpose, our ideal, and how we deal with difficulties. When people say nasty things about us, we might want to immediately respond in a nasty way, but we are guided by a purpose that teaches us to temper our anger with love. When we see members of our church do foolish things, we momentarily lose hope that we can ever build a rational, caring world. We ourselves face moments when the task seems too great, our shortcomings too numerous, and the world too cruel. And so we despair.

I know of no member who does not face these challenges. To succeed as members of the Unification movement we must become people of physical health, mental health, and spiritual maturity. Sometimes I am asked how such and such a person could have left our movement. Sometimes I wonder how anyone is strong enough to continue the quest and remain.

4 / Prisoner Number 596

For those of us building the spiritual community, a great source of strength is the example of the founder of our church, the Reverend Sun Myung Moon. Although Onni did not meet Reverend Moon until 1965, five years after she joined the church, I was able to meet him in December, 1972, just five months after my initial involvement with the movement. My heart was already open to him, for I felt I already knew him through his teachings. Indeed, his emphasis has always been that human beings must be people of principle, not followers of personality.

When I heard that Reverend Moon was actually coming to San Francisco in December of 1972, I did not think much about it, for he was not coming to make a public speech. I was surprised, however, when Onni asked me whether I would like to have dinner with him and a number of other guests at the Sacramento Street Unification Church in San Francisco. On the night of the dinner, I took the most beautiful plant in my home, a flowering bromelia, and brought it with me to present to Reverend and Mrs. Moon.

A Catholic priest, a lawyer, a professor, and several Koreans were sitting in the living room when I entered. When Reverend and Mrs. Moon came into the room we all stood to greet them. They shook hands with the Western guests and bowed to those from Korea. We then proceeded to the dinner table, where my eyes were shocked to discover plates of raw fish. As dinner proceeded, I gulped down a few pieces of raw tuna wrapped in rice, hoping to avoid any taste and desiring to show the breadth of my worldliness or the insouciance of my spirituality. Fortunately, there was plenty of rice and vegetables on the table so I was not called upon to show any more gustatory courage.

Reverend Moon was very attentive during dinner, for he listened with great interest to all of us who, almost compulsively, shared with him everything of interest to us about the United States. His concentration, focus, and quiet reserve struck me more than anything else. His dark brown eyes twinkled, and when he was pleased his entire face lighted up with a broad, expressive smile. Since I valued quiet, courtesy, and kindness, I was not disappointed to find that he and Mrs. Moon showed an abundance of these qualities. I was not looking for spiritual showmanship, so I was not disappointed with people who could listen. Of course, neither Reverend and Mrs. Moon were fluent in English at this time, and when they spoke to express their gratitude, it was through an interpreter.

Reverend Moon was to come to California many times in 1973, and as I became more involved in the church, although I was still working full-time as a professor, I met with him at each visit. We shared many meals, and I was to learn that he could speak about many things as well as listen. Perhaps the central theme of his discourse, and of his teaching, then as well as now, is to have faith in God's principles and to reflect God in His eternal and unchanging quality. When we had breakfast, for example, Reverend Moon would speak to the four of us gathered around the table for four or five hours about God, His principles, and our responsibility. We would then go for a walk. As I took Reverend and Mrs. Moon to one of my favorite spots, the botanical garden in the Berkeley Hills, Reverend Moon would continue his conversation about God by making reference to the creation.

"What is it," he would say, "within the acorn that moves to make the magnificent oak tree? It is a force of mind, of lawfulness, of beauty, but ultimately of love. God is the original force." He would continue, "He is that original mind, and He is that original love. We are, then, standing on holy ground, so let us praise our Creator." Then he would slap me on the back like a Zen master awakening his pupil from a mindless stupor.

Our conversation would continue as we drove across Golden Gate Bridge to the top of the hills in Marin County, overlooking San Francisco Bay. Reverend Moon would always allow me to take him to my favorite place first, but then invariably would ask to be taken to the highest point in the area, where he would then pray to God. As we would often go to the hills in Marin County, I would ask him about human suffering, for it was his understanding of this subject that made me feel especially close to him. My entire life, through the study of literature, psychology, and religion, has been at its heart an attempt to understand the nature of suffering and how to end the tragedy of human history. My name "Durst" means "thirst" in German, and indeed my life has been a thirst to understand. In Reverend Moon I found a man with a similar thirst, but also a man with much understanding.

"We are made for each other," he would say, "to

love, honor, and cherish each other. If we resemble God, as the Bible teaches, then we must resemble Him in that we are able to love. Love is the core of life. It is the motivating force for the desire to know, feel, and act. To love well," he would go on, "is to know the ethics of love. We must be mature and lawful in our love if our love is to bring us joy. If we don't know the law of love, then we cause great suffering instead of great joy. Why do we exploit the environment? Why do we abuse each other? Why do we suffer unnecessarily? Because we do not know how to love in a mature way."

As I came to know Reverend Moon personally, I asked every Korean about his history and that of the Unification Church. I then realized that the teaching I had come to treasure came from a man whose experiences were broad, powerful, and deep. For the first time, too, I realized the importance of an idea to the context in which it is lived.

Although Reverend Moon's life has been filled with pain, suffering, and persecution, the meaning that he has sought to give to his experience has been one of constant faith in God and His principles, and a commitment to reflect God in His eternal and unchanging quality. Here is a man who grew up in poverty, who was imprisoned and tortured numerous times by totalitarian governments, and who has been vilified by the public media in virtually every country he has visited. Yet his response to all of these barbarisms has been the same: forgive, love, and unite.

Reverend Moon was born on January 6, 1920, in what is now North Korea. He was the second son of a farmer whose family converted to Christianity when Reverend Moon was 10 years old. All those who knew

him as a child have testified to his profound seriousness
about the suffering of the world. His immediate family
was trapped in North Korea at the outbreak of the Korean War, and all contact has been lost with them, as is
the case with many thousands of Korean families. His
cousins have told me how, as a young boy, he would ask
God many questions in prayer. At the age of sixteen, on
Easter Sunday morning, Reverend Moon was in
prayer when the spirit of Jesus came down to him and
said: "The mission for the accomplishment of God's
will on earth has been unfulfilled. You, now, must be
responsible for the accomplishment of that misson."

This particular prayer was one of the most deeply
moving of Reverend Moon's life. But he knew that if
the meaning of the vision was to be understood fully, he
would have to pray more powerfully, to study more seriously, and to act with greater focus on a religious
ideal. For the next nine years then, he embarked on the
classical spiritual path of devotion, study and service.
Profound religious conviction, not cheap spirituality,
has always been the foundation of his wisdom.

During the years 1941-44 he attended school at
Waseda University in Tokyo. Since the Japanese had
occupied Korea for many years, and sought to destroy
all of Korean culture, Waseda was the foremost university that would accept Koreans. At Waseda, however,
he was able to pursue with full vigor his religious quest.
A schoolmate and church member, Mr. Duk Moon
Aum, tells of visiting his room:

Father was always very studious, and when I went
to his room I saw Japanese, Korean, and English
Bibles on his desk; many passages had been un-

63

derlined and the margins filled with notations. On Sundays I never found Father home, because he always went to a Christian church, no matter how bad the weather was that day.[1]

Although he sought in Japan to understand the nature of God and the purpose of life in a studious way, he did not keep himself from political action. Soon after arriving in Japan he joined an underground liberation movement that sought to bring freedom to his Korean homeland. Several times he was arrested by the Japanese police and, when he refused to disclose information about the underground movement, he was beaten and tortured. In August 1945, after the American defeat of Japan, Korea was liberated, and Reverend Moon decided to return to Pusan, South Korea.

Upon returning to Korea in 1945, he made further preparations for his ministry. He married and began making his family into the God-centered ideal of husband and wife in service to God and humanity. Later, this first wife would divorce him after seeking to destroy the work of his church. She was wildly jealous of the time that Reverend Moon would spend with church members and church activities rather than with her.

In 1946, as refugees were streaming from the north of Korea to the south, Reverend Moon went north to teach about God; he wanted to confront the godless ideology of communism with his understanding of and his personal relationship with God. He arrived at Pyongyang in June of 1946. Here in the heart of communist North Korea, in a city that at one time had so many churches that it was called the Jerusalem of the East, Reverend Moon began his ministry. He began to teach about God's purpose, God's ideal, and God's love. Many people were attracted to the man and his teaching and, although religious teaching was not yet forbidden by the authorities, Reverend Moon's activities were in complete disfavor with the North Korean communists.

Finally, on August 11, 1947, Reverend Moon was arrested by North Korean authorities. Once again, as with the Japanese police, he was beaten, tortured and this time left for dead outside the walls of the prison in Pyongyang. He was found by his followers, however, and with the help of prayer and herbal medicine was nursed back to life. As soon as he was well enough to talk, he began again to teach his message. This time even more were attracted to what they heard. Numerous members of traditional churches, realizing that something was lacking in their own faith, began to follow Reverend Moon. Irate ministers began writing letters to communist authorities about the danger of Reverend Moon's activities, and on February 22, 1948, he was once again arrested on the charge of advocating social chaos. On April 14, 1948, he was sentenced to five years in Hungnam concentration camp in North Korea. No longer was he Reverend Sun Myung Moon, but Prisoner 596.

Reverend Won Pil Kim, the oldest member of the Unification Church, a follower of Reverend Moon from the days in Pyungnam, describes the situation in Hungnam:

> For the first three months he [Reverend Moon] gave away half the portion of his meal to others, and he determined that he had to survive for five

years with half the food ration. Some prisoners in the same room died while eating, because they were starved. . . .

There were piles of fertilizer from before the war, but they had become as hard as rock because nobody used them during the war. The prisoners had to dynamite them to pieces to pack them into bags. The fertilizer was nitrogenous. . . . They organized ten people into one team and there was a work quota, as is usual in a communist society. When the quota was not fulfilled, they halved the already small amount of food.

Gradually, Father's hands became chapped and torn and started bleeding. Nobody thought that medical treatment was necessary; they only thought of how to finish thirteen hundred bags a day. Father told me he could see his bones. Ammonium sulphate penetrated the wounds; the pain was indescribable.

It was such hard work that the prisoners, dressed only in trousers, were dripping sweat. In this situation Father caught malaria. . . .[2]

Perseverance, endurance, and an incredible will to serve God's purpose allowed him to endure almost three years in Hungnam. Most prisoners did not live past the first. Death seemed imminent for Reverend Moon, too. As United Nations forces were approaching the area of Hungnam in the autumn of 1950, Number 596 was told to prepare for execution. However, on October 14, 1950, U.N. forces arrived at Hungnam and liberated all the prisoners. With Won Pil Kim, and a Mr. Pak, Reverend Moon started the journey back to South Korea on November 4, 1950. Since Mr. Pak had broken his legs and could not walk, Reverend Moon carried him on his back when he could not be pushed by bicycle. Won Pil Kim writes that:

> Taking along a person with a broken leg, Father was risking his life. But to Father, Mr. Pak was more than an individual; he was a representative of all mankind. From God's point of view, all mankind is in a sense crippled.
>
> Even in the very cold winter weather, Father was sweating as he pushed the bicycle. At the foot of a hill, we stopped to rest, even though the sun was still shining. The guns of the Red Chinese army could be heard in the distance.[3]

To celebrate his release from captivity and express his faith in God, Reverend Moon wrote the song "Blessing of Glory":

The light of Glory shines on us from afar,
Revive in strength, you Sacred Spirits of freedom.
These hills and streams, even those valleys awake.
Eternally radiate the reviving light.

He has called us together to realize His glorious existence.

His greatness encompasses the universe.
As he searches for those awakened Sacred Spirits,
How can I attend this Lord?

67

I have awakened from death. When I am embraced
In the bosom of He who woke me,
I rejoice eternally in His eternal love and words
Be joyful eternally and praise His glory.

It was by His grace that I could be embraced,
It is also by His grace that I can be wrapped
To try to return this blessing to Him on high,
That my heart is so unworthy!

Won Pil Kim, Mr. Pak, and Reverend Moon left
Pyongyang on December 4, 1950, and arrived in Pusan, a city in the southernmost part of South Korea, on
January 27, 1951. Although for most refugees the trek
south took between ten days and two weeks, Reverend
Moon's party traveled for almost two months, since
Mr. Pak had to be carried most of the trip. Reverend
Moon would establish his first church in Pusan, and in
this church he would begin to systematize the teaching
of the Unification Church, in his revelation entitled *Divine Principle*.

When I speak of this first church, I am always reminded of the photograph that depicts it so clearly.
From old cardboard refuse left by the American forces,
as well as from scraps of tin, Reverend Moon con-
structed tiny room-like quarters that he dedicated to
God. Several years ago I drove with Reverend and
Mrs. Moon from Seoul to Pusan. In my joy of being
along for the ride, I had forgotten the significance of
Pusan. As we approached a hillside section of the city, I
noticed a large group of people gathered for what
looked like a festival. There were bright-colored

streamers hanging from buildings, men and women wore badge-like insignias with official looking stamps, and children were running to and from, making a loud hullaballoo.

Reverend Moon's car approached a new, recently decorated building, and it appeared that he was about to commemorate something. We got out of the car, entered the building, and stared at a huge glass covering a large brown rock. I thought, "Of course, this is the rock upon which Reverend Moon built his first church; the cardboard and tin church was built next to this rock. My God, he started here! With nothing! and he actually believed that he could comfort God and bring God's redemptive love to the world. He had the hope, even though very few people were with him, that the world would be moved by his love." I realized how I myself was moved by his love, thousands of miles away and years later.

Won Pil Kim describes how he and Reverend Moon first lived in this small church building in 1951 and how the *Divine Principle* was written:

> As soon as he woke up in the morning, Father would start writing, and after he had written a few pages, I would read them back to him, and he would make corrections and additions. We did this every day for a few days. . . .
>
> Once, very early in the morning, Father woke me up and told me to light the lamp and prepare paper and pencils. Except for that one lamp, everything was dark. Father instructed me to write down what he was going to say, and then he dic-

tated the chapter about the Second Coming.

Father didn't stop until he had finished the entire chapter. Usually an author will write down a portion and read it over, reflect on it, and make corrections before going on. But Father dictated without a pause and finished the whole chapter in one sitting. It seemed to me as if Father were reading aloud from a book, since he spoke without stopping, from beginning to end.[4]

The quality of church life in this first, small, cardboard and tin room was to become a prototype for Unification Churches throughout the world. At first, someone would hear about an unusual place where people talked about God, sometimes all night long. One or two people would be seen meditating or praying at all hours of the night. Often, songs and joyful laughter would emanate from the small building. Slowly, guests would come to inquire about what was going on, they would listen to Reverend Moon's teachings, they would return to listen to more, and the congregation would grow.

Just as in Pyongyang, people received so many blessings from God that at night they wouldn't want to leave the church and return to their homes, so we built a small tent in the garden where people could stay and pray all night.

There was a certain pattern by which members were restored: First they heard some kind of rumor about the church, then came and visited it, listened to Principle, and accepted it. Feeling resurrected, they would remain for hours on end at the church, even spending the night there. As a result, opposition would develop. This pattern from Pyongyang was repeated in Pusan.[5]

I have often been with Reverend Moon and felt the joy of his teaching. Listening to him, I have literally felt like I was being "teased into eternity." In a church or on a mountain walk, I am always moved deeply by the reality of God as I listen to him. I remember a trip with him a few years ago, when we traveled to Mt. Surak National Forest with several Korean and Japanese church elders. We started to walk up a trail to the top of Mt. Surak. Together there were about twenty-five men and women, with Reverend and Mrs. Moon in the lead. The last two hundred yards up the face of the mountain, was a sort of granite staircase almost straight up. We began climbing, by this time getting tired. It was a lovely autumn day, and Reverend Moon was indefatigable.

As we reached the top of the granite face, I noticed a cave with an enormous statue of Buddha looking out of the mountainside. I looked behind me and saw my wife talking with the other ladies; they were laughing and enjoying the walk, while some of the men were also talking and laughing. All of a sudden I looked at the Buddha and saw in his eyes the stillness that signifies eternity. I listened to the laughter, and then looked at Reverend Moon. I felt then that what he sought to bring to the world was not the stillness of eternity, but the laughter that would fill it. It was at that moment that time and eternity came together for me. I looked at

Reverend Moon and he was laughing and talking. It seemed he was a man who sought to bring Heaven to earth, and paint earth with the primary colors of love. This memorable experience was like an epiphany, when a wholeness of harmony and radiance suddenly shone forth.

The church in Pusan had grown considerably when in September of 1953 Reverend Moon went to Seoul, the capital of South Korea, to continue his ministry. On May 1, 1954, the Holy Spirit Association for the Unification of World Christianity was established. The Unification Church was formally born. It was not then, nor is it now, Reverend Moon's desire to establish a new Christian sect or denomination. Rather, he seeks through the unity of Christian churches to establish a foundation for the unity of all faiths centered upon God. We speak of the Unification movement more than the Unification Church, for we seek to establish the reality of one human family under God.

The pattern of church growth in Seoul followed that of Pyongyang and Pusan. As most people were ignorant of what was being taught in this new church, rumors spread like weeds in the grass. One rumor was that a man who studied electrical engineering was the minister of the Seoul church. He invented a special apparatus, according to rumor, that would hold anyone who came near it. Hence, those who entered the church could not leave.

Mrs. Gil Ja Eu, another early member of the Seoul church, tells of an extraordinary rumor spread around 1955. The church supposedly had three doors that one had to pass through before entering the central meeting hall. One had to remove, so the rumor went, an article of clothing as one passed through each door, so that presumably one entered the final hall completely naked. One courageous Christian lady came prepared, dressed in three layers of underwear, to find out the validity of this. She of course experienced nothing of what she expected, but instead listened to the church's teachings. She later became a member.

Remarkably, as sophisticated as the United States is, the rumors that spread here about our church in the 1970s paralleled those in Korea. There were articles about how one who entered our church building would be immediately hypnotized by people with glazed eyes. If one ate even one meal in a Unification church center, critics maintained, one would either be drugged or made mindless because of carbohydrate glut. Cartoons depicting our members as robots or puppets and Reverend Moon as the puppetmaster have filled the most popular newspapers and magazines.

Church membership grew in Seoul, as elsewhere in the world, because people came to see for themselves what was happening. They found the rumors were false and that what they heard in the teachings was true. Moreover, they found a community filled with a spirit of joy, love and serious dedication to an ideal. As more and more were attracted to the Unification Church, however, many other traditional social institutions reacted negatively.

Mrs. Eu tells of how many students and professors at Ehwa University, the largest women's university in Korea, were attracted to the church in 1955. Ehwa was founded and funded by the Methodist Church. When numerous students and several outstanding professors became Unification members, they were given an ultimatum: Leave the Unification Church or leave Ehwa University. Mrs. Eu writes:

> ...fourteen of us were called to the office of the dean of students. The dean told us, 'The Unification Church is heresy, and they dance around in the nude. You musn't go there.' We answered, 'We haven't even danced fully clothed, much less nude. If we wanted to dance, we would go to a dance hall. Why should we go to church to dance?' But she said, 'That's not true. You don't know because you're not in very deeply yet. If you keep going, they will make you take your clothes off and dance.'[6]

All fourteen women chose to leave Ehwa University, a great hardship and sacrifice for them, rather than to leave the Unification Church.

The persecution of the church, as it grew quickly in Seoul, culminated in the arrest of Reverend Moon and four other church leaders on July 4, 1955. Twenty days after the arrest, Reverend Moon was charged with draft evasion. Since, however, he was imprisoned in a North Korean concentration camp during the war, he could not have been available for conscription by the South Korean army. On October 4, 1955, he was released, and on November 21, the Korean Court formally declared him not guilty.

The late '50s in South Korea was a time of church growth. Pioneers were sent by Reverend Moon to al-

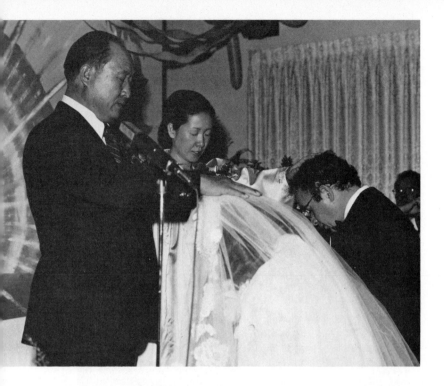

(above) Rev. and Mrs. Moon officiating at the marriage of Dr. and Mrs. Durst in Los Angeles. (below left) At McDonald's in 1974. From left to right; Dr. Durst, Rev. and Mrs. Moon, Mrs. Won Pak Choi, and Onni. (below right) The ocean is an important facet of church life. Here Rev. Moon instructs seminary students in the art of net making, 1978.

(left) Rev. Moon with Dr. and Mrs. Durst in Northern California. (center) Dr. and Mrs. Durst at a church Holy Ground outside Seoul, Korea. (below) The famous Boonville retreat where the only thing ever "locked in" was the fog!

most every city in the nation, and although the church prospered, the pioneers offered themselves as sacrifices for the sake of God and the nation. "Much walking, much persecution, and little food," writes Mrs. Eu, was the life of the pioneer.

In 1957 the first president of the Unification Church of Korea, Mr. Eu, wrote *Explanation of the Principle,* an elaboration of Reverend Moon's revelations, which later became the basis for the English version of *Divine Principle.* Since many concepts in the Korean language do not translate easily into English, there have been a number of English translations of the *Divine Principle.* Although the essential ideas are presented clearly in each, the depth of the concepts varies in precision. Therefore, there is a need for constant examination and revision of translations.

As the church was firmly established in Korea by 1957, in 1958 Reverend Moon sent Mr. Sang Ik Choi as the first missionary to Japan. The pattern of church growth followed by persecution continued in Japan as in Korea. This time as the church grew it would face the formidable enemy of the Japanese Communist Party. Eventually, hundreds of anti-Unification Church articles would appear in *Akahata,* the Japanese communist publication. The communists said that the Unification Church was actually founded by the Korean CIA, that it was not a religion, that it was not even a cult but a business to cheat the public. As an organization that sought to expose the false ideology of communism, the Unification Church was, and still is, a prime target for all communist organizations.

On February 2, 1959, Dr. Young Oon Kim, one of

the professors dismissed from Ehwa University (she is now a professor of religion at our own Unification Theological Seminary in New York) was sent by Reverend Moon as the first missionary to the United States. Several months later, on September 18, 1959, David S. C. Kim, now president of the seminary, came as the second missionary. Where for so many decades Europe and America had sent missionaries to the East and South, now a new movement would bring sweetness and light back to the West.

In 1960 the entire Unification movement celebrated the marriage of Reverend Moon to Hak Ja Han. This marriage of now twenty-four years is an example to Unification members of a family dedicated to establishing God's ideal upon the earth. The love of husband for wife, the respect of children for parents (Reverend and Mrs. Moon have thirteen children) and the loyalty of parents to God's ideal is a model of what we members want to create in our own lives.

Mr. Sang Ik Choi, Kenji (Daikon) Ohnuki, and Onni, because of their success in Japan, came to the United States as missionaries in 1965. This was the year too, that Reverend Moon first visited the United States as part of a world tour of forty countries. This was the tour on which he dedicated 120 prayer grounds or holy grounds, places especially dedicated to God. He would return to the United States on December 18, 1971, and plan his work here.

For Reverend Moon and members of the Unification Church, the United States is a special nation in God's providence. It is a nation that has received abundant blessings: spiritually, politically, and materially. But as it has been given much, we believe, much is expected of it. Reverend Moon came to America to remind this nation of its original ideals, and to urge its people to be an example of God-centered service and love to the rest of the world. On October 21, 1973, in Washington, D.C., during one of his many speaking tours here, he said:

> It is America's position to say to the communists, 'What are you talking about? God exists. God dwells right here with us.' Is America taking this position? No! Today's America is quickly turning self-centered and away from God. America doesn't seem to care about the rest of the world. But you must give America to the rest of the world as a champion for God.[7]

In December of 1973 Reverend Moon came to San Francisco to speak at the Opera House. He and his wife stayed at the church on Washington Street, and I was invited for lunch there the day before his speech. By now I had introduced him to the delights of bagels, so I didn't have to worry about raw fish for lunch. After lunch, he invited me to his sitting room. He began by asking me about marriage, and whether I thought I was serious enough to be married, and whether I understood that the purpose of marriage was to establish a dwelling place for God. After a conversation of several hours, he asked me whether I would consider Onni for my wife. I was ecstatic. When I could speak, I said yes. I then went down to the living room, and Onni was asked to go upstairs to visit with Reverend Moon. I waited for what seemed like forever until I was asked to go upstairs again. Mrs. Won Pok Choi, another of the professors who was forced to leave Ehwa University and who is now the principal of the Little Angels School in Korea, was the translator. Reverend Moon, in a very parental way, spoke to Onni and myself about the seriousness of marriage. Finally, he asked us whether we would consider an engagement for marriage. We both said yes. Several weeks later we were married in our Pasadena, California church when all the leaders of our American church were gathered for a conference.

As with the church in Korea and Japan, the Unification movement in the United States grew rapidly in only a few years. From 1972 until 1976 thousands joined the church as hundreds of thousands came to hear Reverend Moon speak from Portland, Maine, to Los Angeles. In 1976 three hundred thousand went to hear him speak at the Washington Monument. In 1975 missionaries were sent to 127 nations. Literally, a worldwide movement was making itself felt on the stage of history. With the extraordinary growth came the inevitable persecution.

During the past few years, I have appeared on hundreds of television and radio programs, and have given numerous newspaper interviews. After all this experience with the media, I can say that their purpose is more to entertain than inform. This is ironic when the subject is one as profound as religion. They have especially entertained the American public with grotesque images of Reverend Moon. Distorted photos of him, with hands raised in a seemingly menacing gesture, are the normal fare. The content of the stories is no less distorted.

In 1975, NBC presented perhaps the first typical

hatchet job on Reverend Moon. Film clips of his public speeches were selected to show what looked to be an obvious fanatic. With deep gutteral voice and flailing hands, Reverend Moon came across in the show as an Oriental despot. Billy Graham often speaks with gestures similar to those of Reverend Moon, but since Reverend Moon does not speak English, he is more easily perceived as a fanatic. The NBC show also had a sinister-sounding narrator read from Reverend Moon's speeches. Curiously enough, the narrator had a Japanese accent and sounded rather like a cross between Gen. Tojo and Peter Lorre. Obviously Reverend Moon was not to be trusted.

I have seen articles describing the vast wealth of Reverend Moon, so vast that it is said each of his children goes to school in a separate limousine. Well, that's not true. When I travel with Reverend Moon he almost always stays in a local church center. In Korea or Japan the local church is well below the standards of a Holiday Inn. When we travel in the United States, we buy bread and lunch meat at a grocery, or more typically we eat at McDonald's. Surprising, isn't it? Reverend Moon loves McDonald's.

Mornings, I usually go for breakfast at East Garden, the church parsonage where Reverend Moon lives. Although we eat at seven o'clock, he has been up praying since five a.m. He arises at 4:30 and, while it is still dark, goes up to a prayer rock on a hill, sometimes taking one of his children with him. In all church centers there is, of course, a sanctuary for prayer, but wherever Reverend Moon stays he chooses a special rock, tree, or garden for prayer.

Over breakfast there is usually a conference with church elders. There are never fewer than ten or twelve people, and sometimes fifty to a hundred, who have come from all over the world to talk to him. He is concerned about each of us and our work. He regularly gives spiritual advice to members and, when asked, offers his blessings on the many projects discussed. He is, at these gatherings, a source of wisdom, inspiration and strength. Several times I have spoken to him, for example, about how hurt and angry I am at how the public abuses our members and our church. His response is always the same: "Forgive, love, and continue to work hard for the sake of others."

Yet the media and public so misunderstand him. He is a Korean and generally speaks in that language. It is unfortunately a harsh language to Western ears. The harshness of the Korean language is part of the problem the American public has with accepting him. When my Korean wife calls out, "Darling, breakfast is ready," our neighbors probably think we are fighting!

We must also face up to the latent racism in America. Here is an Oriental, a yellow man, attracting and leading bright, capable Americans. Certainly that stirs some people's feelings! We in the West like to believe that only we are capable of bringing advantage to other cultures. It is difficult for American men and women to believe that someone from a "backward" country like Korea could possibly have anything to say to such advanced, modern people as ourselves. Most of those who are hostile to Reverend Moon have never read or even heard one word from him directly.

Yet it is the message of Reverend Moon that stirs up

the most vehement opposition. Here is a clear call to the spiritual life, to put religion first in a day of deep-seated materialism, hedonism, and sensualism. Many cannot believe that anyone will willingly turn away from doing "whatever feels good," from promiscuous sex, alcohol, and drugs to instead serve God and humanity. To such people, those who embrace a self-sacrificing religion must have the power of some sort of mystical, incomprehensible mind control.

For my part, I am inspired by Reverend Moon. He works with church leaders all day until very late at night. I have never seen him turn in before midnight or one a.m. I've seen him preach, teach, lecture ten or more hours at a time, often right through the night. For me and many others, his prayer, his devotion, his constant thought for the members and for the world, and his dedication to reducing the suffering of God, are the truth about him.

There are many sides to Reverend Moon, and one seldom seen by the public is his humor. I have often been touched by his sense of the comic and the picaresque. I hope someday to select even from his sermons an anthology of Reverend Moon's humor. It is a most cosmic humor in that he often attempts to make God laugh. I suppose that the ultimate comfort of God is in being made to laugh, and I think that Reverend Moon tries, not only with passionate tears, but with loving laughter, to comfort Him.

One evening at East Garden, the church parsonage, I was having dinner with him and a number of attorneys working on his tax case. While sitting at the table he said, "We really have to get close to each other, we really have to work together as a harmonious team." He looked at one of the lawyers, grabbed his tie, rubbed his hair, and said, "We should feel this close. You should be able to grab me like this, and I should be able to grab you like this!" Everybody laughed. Reverend Moon was not about to let a serious report obstruct his close, human relationship.

He then spoke in a more serious vein: "Well, fine, whatever happens, ultimately we're religious people. All we can do is to forgive and to love those who have persecuted us. The most important thing is to build something for the future. We need an international judicial system. We need an international standard of justice."

As the attorneys were about to leave after the dinner, Reverend Moon spoke to them at the door. "I know you have been working hard, but I, too, have been working, in New England." He was speaking of the special guidance he was giving to our members in the Unification Church project called Ocean Church, in which young people are encouraged to develop their character through fishing. "I must give you this souvenir," he said as his wife came from the kitchen dragging, one at a time, three fifty-pound striped bass. He gave one to each lawyer. The fish were wrapped up and laid on the carpet. As Reverend Moon opened the wrappings, the lawyers stared incredulously at the striped bass. They then went away in their lovely suits and their Mercedes, with bags full of fish. Reverend Moon was laughing at the door as they left.

For me the most ordinary, and yet most significant experiences with him are the daily ones. Breakfast, for instance, is not just an eating of food, it is a constant conversation about God and the religious life. He is always talking about God, and he acts in such a way as to inspire others to think about God's situation. His words are meant to inspire, to guide and instruct the elders of the church as to how to end God's ancient grief.

One morning, for example, he spoke to me in a very typical way about how in the beginning Adam and Eve cried for themselves when they were cast out from the Garden, cast away from God. Now, however, we must cry for God and mankind in order to be restored to God. Man fell because his thoughts were centered upon himself. The question then is: Can I elevate myself to the point of crying for God and for the world? When I laugh, for example, it should be for God and the world, not arbitrary, or indifferent, or self-centered laughter. When I cry it must be for God and the world. But this sensibility, he went on, is not easy to develop, for it requires self-sacrifice.

Reverend Moon knows that our church could have more members if we were only interested in membership. He is not a fool. He could give joyful talks that merely comfort people. But the central message of the Unification movement is that God suffers, the world suffers, and that it is through sacrifice, through offering ourselves in service to God and in service to the world, that we can end this suffering.

Reverend Moon constantly evaluates himself: How often have I shed tears for the sake of God and for humanity? To be a responsible member of the Unification Church one cannot just fill out a form, but rather must sacrifice one's entire self in service to God and humanity. In the early days, our church used to be called the

Church of Tears, for anyone who is truly a member of the Unification movement must have an awareness of sacrifice.

One wonders: What is the magic this man has that people are automatically drawn to him? He has a special, powerful love as he expresses the heart of God. When the heart of God and the heart of Reverend Moon become one, it is natural for people to be drawn to him.

If one were to ask the question, "Who in the world talks most about God?" I can't imagine anybody talking more about God, feeling more about God, than Reverend Moon. He has a genuine desire to become a loving, serving, giving, healing human being. In a recent sermon entitled "Who is God and Who Am I," Reverend Moon said:

> Why did you come here and sit on the floor? The difference is that this is a public-minded place. We pursue public-minded love because that is where God comes to dwell. To attract God to us we have to live a public-minded life. Last year some eminent professors came to see me at East Garden. One of them was a former Harvard professor, who said proudly to me, 'I am the first Harvard professor to become a Moonie! What can I do?' I answered him, 'I'll tell you what you can do, go out to the world, be persecuted and cursed and give your life for the sake of the world. This is the *Principle*.' The professor might have expected me to compliment him, but not so. The heavenly declaration is to go out and receive persecution, be con-

demned and die for the sake of the world. That Principle is the same for you, for the professor, for the president of the United States. If the president came to me and asked that question, I would give him the same answer. The tombs of people who die for the sake of God and mankind will never be dry. For generations people will come with flowers and shed tears there.

Without any hesitation I will let you go and suffer. God loves the world and He has many problems to bear in the world. Go to Him and say, 'God let me have the worst problem. I will solve it for You.' Now God's greatest headache is atheistic communism. Another headache is the decline of the Christian spirit. Go out to the world and revive Christianity; you be the true revived Christians. Another great headache for God is moral decline, particularly among young people. So go out to the world. Tell God you want to take that headache away by restoring the young people. Americans are individualistic and selfish. Become an example by serving the world, suffering for the sake of others. Because you do it people will say you are brainwashed. Why? You can reply, 'We are resurrected. We are the new breed of people, who hate injustice.' No one wants to suffer, that's human nature. But I am asking you to go down into suffering. . . . The third principle we must practice is sacrifice. Why? Again, the love of God dwells with you if you sacrifice. Sacrifice with love, give yourself to others with love, then you shall win everything there is. From the human standpoint Jesus Christ was miserably defeated. He was crucified and ridiculed by the Roman soldiers. Yet that same Jesus conquered the world because he sacrificed with love. There are many people who have died more miserable deaths than Jesus, but that didn't bring salvation to anyone, because they died for their own cause, or their own crimes. But Jesus did not have any sin, yet he died for the sake of the world with love. That is a true sacrifice. That love conquered the world. Amazingly, when you are conquered by love, you don't hate that conquest. When you become a prisoner of love, you sing and dance.

The three principles I have talked about this morning are points that a noble religious teaching always emphasizes: (1) you should follow the heavenly principle; (2) you should be public-minded; (3) you should be sacrificial. Why? That is where the love of God shall come to dwell. That is the only way we can attract the infinite love of God. Therefore, you don't need someone looking over your shoulder to see whether you are doing it or not. You are bound by your own will, not someone else's. My life was so hard many times that I wanted to quit. But I couldn't. No one else forced me to go on. I kept going because I had tasted the love of God. When you experience the deeper love of God you can't for one moment go away from it.

From evangelistic work in a communist land, to hard labor in a concentration camp, from war and poverty to success in ministry, all of this was accomplished by faith and work. Reverend Moon has faced legal problems in Korea and has been vindicated. He faces legal problems in America, where I believe he will be victorious. The prophet is always rejected, always stoned. But the prophet, if he has the spirit of God, is also always proved right. Love, God's love, can and will conquer all.

During the year of his trial in New York, Reverend Moon comforted us, his friends and lawyers. We did not comfort him! How I loved him when, after the vindictiveness of the courtroom proceedings, he took us to McDonald's and sought to comfort us. Even when the verdict came down "Guilty!" and I burst into tears, he laughed and said, "Don't worry; no problem."

I can see him in my mind's eye now, praying at his prayer rock for hours. I hear him in my mind's ear, speaking for hours on end of the love of God. I know he drives himself. I know he feels the suffering heart of God and longs to comfort Him. I want to join him in that task.

5 / The Teaching Church

As much as I and those of us in the Unification Church admire Reverend Moon, we are taught by him to be people who embody principles rather than ones who blindly follow personality. Reverend Moon, above all, is the embodiment of what he teaches, but it is what he teaches that guides our lives. A nationwide survey conducted of our membership reveals that a great appeal of the Unification movement is its theology. Members are attracted to a rational, systematic worldview. Furthermore, the survey points out many, were social activists in the late 1960s and early '70s. Our members are people who want to practice their ideals. The teaching sets forth ideals for the healthy person, the mature family, the creative community, and the peaceful world. These are ideals that have always moved people, and they speak to the deepest needs within each of us. It is no mystery, then, that the Unification movement has attracted thousands of people in the United States in only a few years.

The first gift Onni put into my hands when I visited the Dana Street house in Oakland was a little book entitled *Divine Principle* (although I have since learned that its Korean title might be better translated *Discourse on Principle*). I didn't ask who the author was, but I took it home and read it. I found myself elevated spiritually, and had a conversion of understanding through the teachings of this revelatory document. Only some time

(above left) Rev. Moon leads a humble church service in Korea. (above right) After liberation from a communist North Korean concentration camp in 1950, Rev. Moon carried his friend Mr. Pak to freedom in the South. (below) In Pusan, South Korea, Rev. Moon built this hut from ration boxes. It was in this building that the *Divine Principle* was first recorded.

(above left) Onni with Rev. Moon in Korea, 1969. (above right) Rev. Moon praying at the Dana St. church in Oakland, California, in 1972. (below left) Onni in June 1973. (below right) At the Oakland Holy Ground, 1972. Left to right; Onni, Mrs. Moon, Rev. Moon, Mrs. Choi, and Michael Runyon.

(above) Dr. and Mrs. Durst. (center) Dr. Durst on his birthday, September 5 1983, with Rev. and Mrs. Moon, and his wife. The group was in Cartagena, Colombia, at the annual media conference. (below) A church seminar in Northern California.

(above) Rev. and Mrs. Moon on an outing with church members in Korea. (below) Dr. Durst receiving the Order of Law, Justice, and Peace from the Mexican Academy of Law, at the United Nations building in 1981.

(above) Dr. Durst at a church celebration.
(below) Speaking at a press conference, 1982.

(above) Rev. and Mrs. Moon with their children and grandchildren, 1983. (center) Dr. Durst at East Garden, the U.S. church home of Rev. and Mrs. Moon. (below) Left to right; Dr. Durst, Onni, Yeon-do, Isaac & Chaim

later did I ask Onni, "Who wrote that book you gave me?" She told me that Reverend Sun Myung Moon received the knowledge contained in *Divine Principle* through study, prayer, and revelation, and that he had suffered persecution for his faith. That statement doubly certified the teachings for me, and yet I was already convinced of the holiness of the message.

"How can we know the characteristics of God, who is an invisible being? We can know them by observing the world of His creation. . . . Just as the work of an artist is a visible manifestation of its maker's invisible nature, every creation is a 'substantial object' of the invisible deity of God, the Creator. His nature is displayed in each creation. Just as we can sense an author's character through his works, so we can perceive God's deity in observing His creation." With these words, I was off on my spiritual journey through the teaching of *Divine Principle.*

By looking at human beings, the *Divine Principle* continues, we find truth-seekers, beauty-seekers, and love-seekers. Our nature is to seek value, and the world just happens to correspond to our needs. It is truthful, beautiful, lovable. We have infinite desire, infinite creativity, and infinite love not to be frustrated, but rather to be infinitely valuable. The challenge of life, however, is to use our mind, heart, energy, and creativity in constructive ways. We must ripen or mature our nature before we can realize our full value. The *Bible* says "be fruitful," then multiply and have dominion. To be fruitful is to mature according to our nature and purpose.

What is our nature? We have a mind that allows us to know truth or reality. The *Divine Principle* explains that our desire to know is ultimately rooted in our heart, the ground of our being, which directs us to love that which we know. So, for example, if we study medicine, we ideally are motivated to heal the human body. If we study law, we ideally are motivated to heal the social fabric. Human beings, then, have developed the sciences by which to observe, to experiment with, and to know this world. Philosophy and religion have been developed to allow us to live well with what we know. The goal of human life, *Divine Principle* explains, is to fulfill our ideals and our love in the largest way possible. We are meant to be fully *human* beings, and thus to say, as with Buddha, "In me you see the fullness of the universe," or as with Jesus, "In me you see the Father."

It is reasonable for us to infer, the *Divine Principle* elaborates, that since we have a mind that seeks to know and a heart that seeks to love, there must be a cause or source for our nature. We speak of this cause as God. Where else could mind come from? Out of what original, white-hot heat of creation could mind come from? Where does love come from? From what material, evolving in what random way, do we get Moses, St. Paul, and Gandhi? Human beings in their nature resemble God in His nature. Indeed, the *Bible* tells us that human beings are created in the image of God.

The ground of God's being, and thus the ultimate ground of all beings, the *Divine Principle* points out, is purposeful love. We seek to know the truth or reality of an existence so that we may connect well with it, be stimulated by it, and love it. We look to perceive and to create beauty because our heart is stirred to love that which is beautiful. In like manner, God seeks to connect with what He creates, so that He may feel the fullness of His own love.

I remember so well how, when I first read this, I felt like I had looked up at the sky and saw stars for the first time. It was not that I was unaware of the infinity of existence, but rather of how I was purposefully related to it. Now, for the first time, I felt intimately connected to the universe. I felt as though I had come home, that it was all right to come home, and that my parents were waiting to embrace me. Recently I was given a small sculpture of the Prodigal Son by Benjamin Bufano, the San Francisco artist. It depicts a father embracing his son so that they form one being. So, too, I felt that God was my personal parent when I understood my relationship to Him.

Onni had told me many times that the purpose of life was to be "a value-maker and a happy-maker" through purposeful love. By reading *Divine Principle* and studying the lectures that accompanied it, I realized that Onni was urging me to resemble God in heart and love. All of my life seemed to come into focus, as I realized that I could use my mind, energy, and love to resemble God's loving nature, and thus to become fully human. I felt like an artist who realized that his own life was the consummate work of art. It struck me that my fascination with art was its beauty and thus its ability to bring joy and consolation to a world filled with suffering. Now I realized that I had to make my life beautiful, through truly ethical action, and thus be a joy and comfort to others.

With my new-found joy, focus, and excitement came a sober sense of responsibility. If I were to become the consumate artist, I had to take responsibility for the direction of my every thought, feeling, and action. No longer could there be an arbitrary or indifferent standard for my activities. Rather, God as the standard of value would represent a universal love, a universal care, a universal heart. I, too, would actively have to seek to build a human community centered on love. The world would now become the Garden I would have to cultivate. The human family, was no longer an abstraction, it became real as I felt the reality of the brothers and sisters around me.

I was powerfully aware of God's universal love when I first studied the teachings of the Unification movement. It was not that I had never heard these ideas before, but that they had never been presented so rationally or "heartistically." Even to this day, I feel moved when I hear Reverend Moon speak about God's love. In a recent sermon he spoke about how

All creation is made to stimulate love. When God looks at His creation, He says, 'It is good.' The perfection of love is the purpose of life. . . . We are born as the prince and princess of love, to become king and queen of love, and to build the Kingdom of love.

If life is the process by which we are to perfect our love, the family is the palace of perfection. With the *Divine Principle* as my guide I had new hope for creating a healthy, loving family as the basis for a peaceful world. Before joining the Unification movement, two of my greatest ideals had been unrealized. I wanted to have a loving family that would be a source of great joy, and I wanted a world without war. Unfortunately, I did not know how to achieve either of these ideals. With the teaching of Reverend Moon and the Unification movement I had clear, if not easy, directions.

I realized that the family unit was the basic structure by which God could realize His ideal (and mine) of a peaceful, loving world. Children had to be taught respect for parents, who could seek to represent God's unselfish and unconditional love to children. If parents sought to resemble God's love, and children sought to follow their parents, then God's love would be the guiding force for family life. The innocence and purity of children would be guided by ethics. The way of love would become the ethic of life.

Along with respect for parents, children would learn the art of brotherly-sisterly love. Older brothers and sisters would learn to care for those who were younger, while those younger would learn to respect the older. Since boys and girls reflect God's masculine and feminine nature, they would mature in such a way as to embody God's parental heart. A mature man would reflect God's universal masculine love, and a mature woman would embody God's universal feminine love. Literally, cosmic man and cosmic woman would come together in marriage. What would be the quality of their love? Well, they would reflect God's love, which is eternal, absolute, and unchanging. As God gives Himself completely to the world, the mature man and woman would exhibit a love that is unselfish and sacrificial.

When Onni and I were married, she soon began calling me her "eternity-mate." "What?" I asked, thinking she was again dismembering the English language. "You know," she replied, "we will be together for eternity and love each other for eternity." As I looked at her I saw a person totally confident about and committed to the words that had come out of her mouth. I began to feel that something that had died within me was being reborn.

Fidelity of husband and wife to each other, the husband living for the well-being of his wife and the wife living for the happiness of her husband, is the ideal of marriage taught in the Unification movement. The family unit, then, would be a model for the larger society. All those in parental positions, like teachers, would feel responsible to raise up young people to an ideal of public service and civic virtue.   Furthermore, all families would seek the well-being of all other families, for God would be recognized as the parent of one human family.

> You . . . must be loving your spouse and as God would have you love your spouse and as God would love your spouse; and in loving your parents, you must be loving them as God would have you love them and as God would love them; and in loving your children, you must be loving them as God would have you love them and as God would love them. If you do that, the children will do the same toward you and their grandparents, and the parents will do the same to reach you and their grandchildren. That is the measure of love, that is the tradition.[1]

Be fruitful, multiply, and have dominion was clearly the blessing given to us by God. The *Divine Principle* clarifies the meaning of biblical blessing and illustrates how that blessing can be realized. Each human being could fulfill his or her purpose by maturing in love. We would thus be "fruitful" as we developed a caring, giving, unselfish love for the entire human community. We could "multiply," and thus receive the second blessing, by entering into marriage and bringing forth children. Finally, we could have the blessing of "dominion" by entering into lawful and loving relationship with all things. This was not to be a dominion of destruction and control, but one of harmonious interaction.

"Be a value-maker and a happy-maker through purposeful love" ran through my mind so many times as I studied the *Divine Principle*. Onni had a way of simplifying complex material by speaking to its essence. "Use your creativity to bring joy to God, joy to the world, and joy to your family," she would say. The creativity of love was the key of life, I thought. What is life other than creative "strategies of love." I felt surging within me the power of religion in its most vital form. I could use all of my energy and all of the energy around me if I could learn to resemble God's lawful and loving creativity. The question of understanding the nature of creativity became central to my desire to use it constructively. Onni then had me reread the section on "The Purpose of the Creation of the Universe" in the *Divine Principle*.

In order to understand more precisely the questions concerning God's purpose of creation, let us first examine how joy is produced. Joy is not created by the individual alone. Joy comes when we have an object, whether invisible or visible, in which our own character and form are reflected and developed, thus enabling us to feel our own character and form through the stimulation derived from the object.

For example, man feels joy as a creator only when he has an object, that is, when he sees the product of his work, whether it be a painting or sculpture, in which his plan is substantiated. In this way, he is able to feel his own character and form objectively through the stimulation derived from the product of his work. When the idea itself remains in the objective position, the stimulation derived from it is not substantial; therefore, the joy derived from it cannot be substantial either. God's joy is produced in the same manner as man's. Therefore, God feels joy when He feels His original character and form objectively through the stimulation derived from His substantial object.[2]

Onni would simplify this discussion of creativity in the following way: "How do we create? Let us assume that we are not just blank slates, but that we are pulsating beings, beings of energy, beings of mindfulness, beings of beauty, and beings of love. Suppose we have an idea for a song in our minds." She would then sing a few lines from Frank Sinatra's "My Funny Valentine" or Patti Page's "Tennessee Waltz." (Onni was listening to *exactly* the same songs in Tokyo that I was listening to in New York.) "The idea itself," she would continue, "gives a certain amount of pleasure. We then get into the shower and start singing. What happens? We have more stimulation. Then what do we want to do? We want to get an orchestra, a band, a microphone, amplifiers, and belt it out! We want greater stimulation. We want to express, to interact, to feel joy."

What happens when someone creates anything with a tremendous investment of energy, heart, and mind? It gives us joy. Why? Because our own mind and heart are stimulated by what an artist has invested of himself.

More than just inventions or works of art, what things give us the greatest joy? Our children, of course. Those in whom we invest the greatest love give us the greatest joy. If we invest our full self in someone, and there is a full response, then there is the greatest joy. In most normal cultures, children give individuals the greatest joy. We look at our child's picture on our desk. We write a postcard to our child if we are ten thousand miles away. We hope our children will be better than we are; I never met a parent who did not hope that his or her child would be more beautiful and more loving than himself or herself. If our children act in such a way that they are truthful, beautiful, and loving, we feel the greatest joy. But if our children act in ungrateful ways, if they are hateful, unloving, unkind, then there is no greater suffering to the human heart.

If we feel joy from what we create, and from our children, our feeling is exactly analogous to what God must feel. The world is charged with the grandeur of God. Everything in creation is a testimony to God, and God creates to experience joy. Human beings are the fullest reflection of God's nature and, thus, as we resemble God, we can bring Him the greatest joy.

God can experience joy! His own being can become joyful if He beholds the beauty of human life, if we humans are truly able to be loving in a divine way. But the contrary is also true. If human beings fail to act in a large or loving way, God suffers. The world suffers. Everyone suffers. And we suffer. When we look at human history, we have to grieve over what people have inflicted on each other. We have acted like vermin rather than like human beings filled with any large kind of love. We have exploited, abused, violated, and perpetrated every kind of viciousness upon the sacredness of human life and the sacredness of this lovely, spinning globe. God's situation is one of ancient grief. Human history is a tragedy, and our own life is a mockery of what we are meant to be.

If the *Divine Principle* clarifies how we are meant to live purposefully in order to receive God's blessings, it also explains how a violation of our purpose and nature causes us to be cursed. When I first understood the fall of humanity, or the root cause for evil and tragedy, I felt as though a heavy curtain had been lifted from in front of my eyes. I had always attributed the cause of evil to greed, hatred, anger, and envy, but I did not understand how even these ignoble qualities were rooted in the misdirection of love.

Love centered upon God, the *Divine Principle* explains, is the source of human life and happiness. To love the world as God loves the world, to care for it as He does, is the foundation for a life of value. To love the world from God's point of view demands, however, that we grow. We have to love as we are guided by an ethical ideal of God-centered love. If, however, we fail to take God as the object of our love, we become idolators and commit every kind of evil.

Good and evil are fundamentally different. Evil asks everything different. Evil asks everything and everyone for himself. It asks everyone to be and exist for himself. But good exists for others. We have to make this clear and understand that this is the dividing point. When we follow this formula for goodness, we become the greatest of all men. If we go the first way, we become dictators. Patriots are those who sacrificed themselves in the interest of their own nation. Saints live not only for man, but for God.

We can see that good and evil start at the same point but head in different directions. Service to others is seemingly good, but unless the service is centered on Godly love, we cannot call it good. So, we cannot deny that good and evil are headed in different directions according to the quality of love they are centered upon.[3]

Self-centered love, immature love, and misdirected love became the source, I was to learn, of breakdown in the family and destruction in the larger society. I thought of my own marriage and realized that the only hope for significant and lasting relationship was profound purpose. I could see all around me how people were attracted to each other, and fall in and out of marriage, because the marriage partners did not live for any meaningful purpose. I would see children disrespecting their parents because they could not respect the purpose for which their parents were living. I thought of the crime that rages throughout New York City and the violence that pervades much of the world, and I could see clearly the failure of loving purpose, the failure of constructive purpose, and thus the lust to destroy.

What was the tragedy of human history, I would ask myself many times while studying the *Divine Principle*, but hatred of individual against individual, tribe against tribe, nation against nation, race against race, religion against religion. When would hatred end? Only when we could learn to love. It was the simplest answer in the world but, as I was to find out, the hardest to practice. Could I genuinely seek to benefit others in all of my actions? This was to become the great challenge of living the tenets of the *Divine Principle*. If God grieves and the human community suffers because of the misdirection of love, could I develop a heart of redemptive love to restore myself to God's original ideal?

The restoration of original value, of God's original ideal, is the purpose of human history, the *Divine Principle* explains. Salvation is the restoration of God's original purpose of creation. Unlike many religions, which believe that salvation is merely personal, or perhaps primarily mystical, the Unification view is that salvation is the restoration of this world to the fulfillment of God's original ideal of the Kingdom of Heaven on earth. That kingdom on earth is a world where God's love reigns as the operational principle of human life. Individuals, families, nations will comprise one family under God. Individuals may still do stupid things, people may still hurt each other, and the New York Yankees may still not win the pennant every year, but God's love will be the overwhelming force guiding human relationships.

The concept of the Last Days, from the Unification point of view, is not one of mystery in which God will magically lift up those who are to be saved and turn away from those who are damned. Rather, it is a time when human beings will exercise their full responsibility in turning away from the selfishness of the past to the God-centeredness of the future. What is needed, Reverend Moon teaches, is a revolution of the heart from selfishness to unselfishness—not a violent revolution of guns and bullets, but a quiet one of human motivation. Even though Jesus taught us to pray "Thy Kingdom come, thy will be done, on earth as it is in heaven," we look around us and see that the world is essentially as rotten as it was two thousand years ago. What Christ taught us to pray for remains unfulfilled. When Jesus appeared to Reverend Moon on Easter Sunday in 1936, he urged the sixteen-year-old boy to take up the mission of establishing God's ideal upon earth. This has been Reverend Moon's life-long mission.

The Messiah, the Lord of the Second Advent, the *Divine Principle* teaches, will be one who appears in this age as a model of God's love to a world that knows little about God and even less about His love. He will be one who seeks to bring unity of religion, race, and culture centered upon God's ideal. He will seek to communicate to the world how God grieves, and how we, as loving sons and daughters, must liberate God's suffering heart by establishing a peaceful world centered on God's love. Through the teaching of the *Divine Principle* I have felt new life. For the first time I feel like God's son, and I am motivated to love my brothers and sisters so that I may comfort Father and Mother (God). Reverend Moon has given me this new life through the teachings of the *Divine Principle*.

6 / The Work of the Church: In Service to God and to Humanity

By 1977, with a fledgling community of committed and dedicated people, and with a sound teaching that inspired us to live our ideals, the Unification movement in California had grown rapidly. Our first challenge was to become ourselves a model of what we wanted the world to become. The love-ethic presented in the *Divine Principle* demanded a life of prayer, study, and service to others. We sought within our community to be caring, creative, and loving people, and upon this foundation to work actively for the sake of God and humanity.

We called ourselves "The Creative Community Project" and used a former fraternity house on Hearst Street as a place to teach the *Divine Principle* at luncheon and dinner programs. We were inspired by an ideal and wanted above all to communicate that ideal to those around us who, so it seemed, had very little commitment to anything other than self-interest.

Most people we encountered had only the foggiest sense of ethics, so we felt great meaning in sharing with them, through our dinner discussions and lectures, the significance of our own ethical ideals. Those who were serious and wanted to pursue those ideals further were invited to workshops at Boonville and, later, to other country retreats.

Hand in hand with teaching was our desire to do substantial good works so that people could *see* that we were serious about making the world a better place. From my experiences at the inner-city college in Oakland, I knew that right in the heart of the city, people had an enormous need for the basic necessities of life. I had the greatest satisfaction in simply helping students with fundamental reading and writing skills to enable them to fill out job applications. Many of them were unemployed, and I knew that what they were eating in the cafeteria was often insufficient. I decided to mobilize our spiritual community to help the larger human community in Oakland.

Since about forty acres of the Boonville farm consisted of an apple orchard and a vegetable garden, and, since every October we harvested such a super-abundance of fruit and vegetables that much of it would go uneaten and rot in the field, I thought: Why not pack this food in crates and distribute it to people in Oakland? We had given some of our harvest to neighbors, but now Jeremiah Schnee and Russell Allen, two stalwarts of our community, and I tried to figure out how we could systematically distribute it to a larger number of people. Jeremiah suggested we look in the telephone book under churches and social service groups, then make calls to the appropriate directors or ministers to see whether they would be willing to take any food. Russell assured us he could get a truck and some of the men to do the distribution. We were on our way, if not to solve the problem of hunger in the world, at least to help some people in our own community.

Although in our first distribution effort we gave

away only a few tons of food, what became known as "Project Volunteer" has since then given away millions of pounds of food, medical supplies, and other needed surplus material. The project has now spread to numerous cities throughout the United States, and last year in Oakland alone the project distributed over five million pounds of surplus government cheese.

After our first distribution from the Boonville farm, we learned that the great central valley of California grows about one quarter of the fruit and vegetables for our nation, and that, as in Boonville, a great part of any harvest would either rot on the vine or in the ground. Wholesalers, for example, would only buy picture-perfect fruit and vegetables for the supermarkets. Any food with even the slightest blemish was culled, placed in thousand-pound bins to be dumped in the ground. We found, too, that growers and wholesalers would have to pay for this good food to be carted off. All this then was happening a few miles from cities in the San Francisco Bay area where people were malnourished.

Our community purchased several trucks and a warehouse in Oakland, not far from the college where I was teaching. We began, under Russell Allen's supervision, to make regular trips to Modesto, Stockton, Vacaville, and numerous farming areas throughout California. Our young volunteers would bring guitars on the trucks and would be accompanied by senior citizens who went along for the gleaning. Truly, the biblical concept of gleaning the fields was being revived.

Several retired men and women built a food-processing room in our warehouse. Then, after we obtained the materials, a retired electrician built a huge refrigerator-freezer next to the dry food storage area. Since refrigerated space was usually expensive, we became one of the few such groups to be able to store fresh vegetables and government surplus butter, milk, and cheese. Our greatest boon came a few years ago when we received several thousand frozen pizzas from a large company. I thought the Kingdom of Heaven had surely arrived.

Through Project Volunteer we sought to embody the *Divine Principle*'s ideal of public service and civic virtue. Of course these are good old Yankee virtues as well, but we felt that words and concepts like *virtue*, *honor*, *nobility*, and *love* had to be revitalized. We did not want people to become dependent on us through our service, rather we wanted to awaken their divine nature and get them to help each other. We gave food and other materials directly to the leaders of various community groups so that they could work with their own people. We did not desire credit for our efforts, and to this day most recipients of material from Project Volunteer do not know that we are involved.

The Creative Community Project, which conducted seminars on the *Divine Principle*, together with Project Volunteer organized numerous activities throughout California. We would travel to Sacramento with musicians to hold a square dance for members of Senior Gleaners, a group of retired men and women who themselves distributed surplus food to the needy. We honored their president, Homer Fahrner, at an awards banquet for volunteers. We held Christmas parties at homes for the elderly in Oakland, and we visited the sick in hospitals throughout the Bay Area. Dr. David Rueter, a podiatrist, opened up a clinic to help the poor, and Sheri Sager Rueter, a registered nurse, would give lectures on "Health for Seniors" in San Francisco. In Los Angeles, where we also eventually bought a warehouse to distribute surplus food, we worked together with eight churches for a Spring Gospel Concert. We felt filled with the spirit of God's love, and wanted to express that in service to our brothers and sisters.

I was very pleased one day in 1976 to receive an invitation from David S. C. Kim, one of the earliest missionaries to the United States, to become a member of the board of a relief organization founded by members of the Unification Church. The International Relief Friendship Foundation[1] (IRFF) was established to provide emergency assistance to people in need throughout the world, and also to assist in long-term development projects that would attack the causes of poverty, malnutrition, and disease. My vision of helping a few poor in Oakland was now being stretched to include the needy of the world.

Over the last few years IRFF has helped people in over 35 countries either through emergency assistance or aid to long-term development projects. We have sent tons of food to Santo Domingo, medical supplies to Zaire, and clothing and material to various refugee groups in Southeast Asia. In Thailand we operate a full-time medical team at the Sikhui Vietnamese refugee camp. "This camp is for boat people who escaped from the communist regime in Vietnam," writes Kem Mylar, secretary general of the IRFF. "However, the

Thai government is concerned that there might be communist agents among them and keeps them separate from the general population. But the IRFF medical team, with its determination to provide medical service, consists of twenty-five to thirty members, eight of them are Unification Church members, including a doctor, a pharmacist, and a laboratory technician.''[2]

In Zaire, members of IRFF established an agricultural and technical school called ECOPROF (L'Ecole Cooperative Professionelle). Kehaulani Haydon, a member of the IRFF staff, explains:

In the first year of preparatory training, students receive a weekly course on 'spiritual values and ethics' in addition to general education, language, mathematics, typing, and other basic subjects. The second and third years continue in the two specializations of the technical cycle: commercial management and fishfarming. Students are also required to complete practical work internships, often in cooperation with other non-profit organizations such as the Peace Corps. These internships give the students an opportunity to apply practical knowledge learned in the classroom to realistic field situations such as constructing ponds and fish cultures and building small bridges.[3]

Nearly simultaneous with the birth of IRFF in 1977 was the organization of the National Council for the Church and Social Action. (NCCSA) NCCSA is a product of the vision of church ministers from over twenty denominations who met at Fordham University in May, 1977. Because of the ecumenical vision of Reverend Moon, which ties in spiritual teaching with practical activities, the Unification Church has supported NCCSA with funding and manpower since its inception. Each chapter of the National Council (there were about forty-five local chapters by the spring of 1984) is independent and is governed by a local board of directors that interacts with the national board. The overall purpose of the organization is to mobilize the resources of a community to serve the spiritual, emotional, and material needs of its poor.

Kevin and Maria Brabazon, members of the Unification Church, were involved in organizing the Harlem Council for Church and Social Action. They live in Harlem and were concerned about the many, many needs of their community. I went to visit them for the first time in the summer of 1980. As I entered their office, which was near their apartment on 125th Street and Amsterdam Avenue, I was struck by the activity of four or five young men and women on telephones writing frantically in what looked like schedule books. Kevin and Maria had set up a transportation system by which elderly people would be picked up at their homes and driven to shopping markets, churches, or hospitals. The project was working so well that Kevin was able to employ a number of young people from the community; also, new passenger vans were donated by the City of New York.

Kevin and Maria are particularly committed to solving the problems of poverty and racism by showing what one couple with a vision can do. They were married by Reverend Moon several years ago, and they take seriously the ideals of the Unification Church. Like so many couples in our movement, theirs is an interacial marriage centered on God's love.

Ronald Johnson, a member of the New York City Council for Church and Social Action, helped organize the Farm Club for residents of Harlem in the summer of 1983. On land in upstate New York they began numerous gardens.

> The most inspiring member proved to be Fanny Freeman of 118th Street. She grew up on a farm in Alabama and learned the value of growing her own food at an early age. A very active urban gardener in recent years, she has prompted many of her neighbors to become community gardeners. When she first heard about the Farm Club there was no holding her back. She would get up early and cook barbequed beef and chicken, corn bread, and collard greens for everyone who came. This feast became a regular feature of our Farm Club, a shared community meal at our Saturday outings. As the season progressed, many of our own vegetables made their way into the picnic lunch.[4]

Project Volunteer, the International Relief Friendship Foundation, and the National Council for Church and Social Action are only three of the humanitarian projects that have developed out of the teaching and vision of Reverend Moon. Another organization inspired by Reverend Moon often co-sponsoring projects with these others, and dedicated to ending racism and religious bigotry, is the Minority Alliance International

(MAI). MAI has hosted annual banquets celebrating the birth of Dr. Martin Luther King, has organized cultural nights at the Manhattan Opera Center in New York, a Unification Church-owned facility, and has organized ecumenical conferences to promote interfaith and interracial harmony.

In May of 1978 I had the pleasure once again of accompanying Reverend and Mrs. Moon to Korea. We stopped overnight in Tokyo and Reverend Moon spoke to church leaders in the morning. Afterwards about twenty-five of us drove to a new gray stone building where several men and women in white laboratory coats and wearing broad smiles were waiting to greet us. Reverend Moon was to dedicate a new hospital.

On a tour of the soon-to-be-opened Isshin Hospital, as we passed from room to room, Reverend Moon would say a prayer and sprinkle sanctified salt. Everything must be dedicated to God, Reverend Moon always taught us. All the while, I couldn't help thinking back to the rock in Pusan and how, with almost nothing, Reverend Moon believed he could create a movement that would be of service to the world. It struck me that most people would consider their lives highly successful if they, like he, could be the inspiration behind the founding of even one hospital.

The philosophy of Isshin Hospital, we were to learn from the woman who was the head doctor, as well as a Unification Church member, corresponded to the teaching of the *Divine Principle*. The doctors sought to work unselfishly for the well-being of their patients and would emphasize in their treatment the prevention of illness. Medical care, we learned, was based on the latest Western medicine, but various techniques of oriental medicine were also available. We saw the latest technology in each area of the hospital: departments of internal medicine, orthopedics, dermatology, pediatrics, plastic surgery, obstetrics, and physical therapy, a dental clinic, and an eye clinic.

The World Medical Health Foundation was incorporated in New York in 1977 as a public, non-profit educational and research organization by a group of medical professionals who were inspired by the philosophy and ideals of Reverend Moon. Though the founding members were all members of the Unification Church, it was hoped that the vision and goals of the medical foundation would attract medically oriented people of many different religious and philosophical persuasions, but who shared the concepts of unified medicine and absolute values, and the ideal of a unified world. The foundation was originally organized through a grant from the International Cultural Foundation, but since then has been entirely self-sufficient through private donations and through offering seminars and classes on a wide variety of topics.

At various times, the medical foundation has offered programs to the general public, and to other health professionals, in the areas of childbirth education, nutrition and dietetics, natural therapeutics, and first aid, with an emphasis on wellness, lifestyle, and preventive medicine. Currently the foundation is offering programs on stress management, weight management, and personal growth.

Dr. William Bergman, a New York physician and a close friend of mine who joined the Unification Church in Oakland, California, while he was working at Kaiser Hospital, is the director of the foundation. A sparkling intellect, deep heart, and joyful smile are the qualities one is struck by on first encountering this Columbia University-trained physician.

Since the teaching of the Unification movement has at its core a commitment to value, it is natural for Reverend Moon to have created numerous activities for scientists, philosophers, and other academicians to focus on ethical questions. The International Cultural Foundation, an organization established in 1968, promotes academic discussion of the highest caliber through the International Conference on the Unity of the Sciences, the Professors World Peace Academy, and the Washington Institute for Values in Public Policy.

The International Conferences on the Unity of the Sciences (ICUS) annually bring together hundreds of intellectuals to discuss the relationship of science to absolute value. The tenth annual conference in 1981 in Seoul, South Korea, gathered almost eight hundred participants from 108 nations. Conference proceedings are published each year, and have become resource material in the area of science and values. At the 11th conference in Philadelphia, the first bienniel Founder's Award was given to Dr. Eugene Wigner, a Nobel Laureate in physics, for his outstanding contributions to science. Dr. Wigner has been a regular committee chairman for these annual conferences.

A cynic might say that Reverend Moon promotes such conferences only because he is interested in giving credibility to the Unification Church. Nothing could be further from the truth. Reverend Moon has spent his life initiating hundreds of activities like the ICUS series because he wants to bring credibility to God and hope to human life. Those hostile to our church criticize our most innocent acts. Were we to help an old woman across the street, they would speculate on where we were taking her and for what nefarious purpose. Well, we have now taken many, many people across the street, and they have gotten safely to the other side.

Another major ICF-sponsored outreach project to the academic world is the Professors World Peace Academy. This group, which exists in more than fifty countries, supports academic research, conferences, and publications dealing with the theme of world peace. I recently participated in a conference sponsored by the PWPA of Japan on "Japan in the 1980s." The current president of the PWPA in the United States is a professor of neuroscience, Karl Pribram, of Stanford University.

The PWPA of the United States recently initiated a Task Force on Central America as an outgrowth of its annual conference on "United States Foreign Policy Options for the '80s." The Central American task force then became a project of the Washington Institute for Values in Public Policy in late 1982. The PWPA is an international association of scholars and academicians dedicated to researching issues affecting world peace. The Washington Institute is an independent, non-profit research and educational organization devoted to providing policy-makers, scholars, and the public with non-partisan analysis of issues affecting the world and nation. A recent book (1983) published by the Washington Institute is entitled: *Central America in Crisis: A Program for Action.* Both the Washington Institute and the PWPA are affiliates of the International Cultural Foundation, but the board of each operates with total independence.

Reverend Moon has also inspired an ambitious publishing program, Paragon House Publishers, to help disseminate vital ideas to the academic world. Selected readings from the Proceedings of the International Conferences on the Unity of the Sciences have been recently published by Paragon. Professor Richard Rubenstein, distinguished professor at Florida State University, edited one volume entitled *Modernization*, and Sir John Eccles, Nobel Laureate in medicine, edited a volume, *Mind and Brain*. The editorial board at Paragon, which operates with complete independence from the Unification Church, is headed by Professor Frederick E. Sontag, the Charles A. Dana Professor of Philosophy at Pomona College in California. Professor Sontag has also written a major scholarly book on Reverend Moon.

It has always been the Unificationists' desire to promote the revitalization of *all* religions along with interreligious cooperation. Reverend Moon teaches us to respect all religions, and we especially look upon Judaism and Christianity as our elder and middle brothers. My vision of the future, Reverend Moon's vision, and, I believe, God's vision is of a world of interracial, international, and interreligious harmony.

To make this a reality, Reverend Moon founded the International Religious Foundation, (IRF) which sponsors numerous interfaith activities. A youth seminar on world religions is one IRF project. Each year approximately one hundred and fifty college students and advisers representing each of the major faiths are chosen to make a pilgrimage to major holy places around the world. The students are accompanied by eminent professors who lecture on different areas of religious history and culture. The purpose of such a seminar is to stimulate young people to examine the nature of the religious experience and then to respect, in William James's phrase, the varieties of religious experience.

The IRF also sponsors the New Ecumenical Research Association (New ERA), composed of hundreds of scholars throughout the world who meet regularly in conferences, publish books, and seek to promote religious dialogue generally. In a recent conference on "God," Professors Sontag and M. Darrol Bryant of the University of Waterloo, Ontario, Canada, made the following comments in an introduction to the published proceedings:

> For a world in religious turmoil, as ours is, the notion of God must be the center of dialogue. Recognizing this, New ERA has inaugurated a series of conferences, to be held annually, on the topic of God. The first of these, "God: The Contemporary Discussion," was held on December 26 - 31, 1981, at Maui, Hawaii, and involved 164 philosophers, religionists, and theologians. The participants represented most of the world's major religious, philosophical, and cultural perspectives. We hope that the high quality of ecumenical discussion begun there can be continued into the future.[5]

In June 1983 the IRF sponsored an Interdenominational Conference for Clergy, in the Bahamas. Over 170 Catholic and Protestant ministers participated in the conference, the central theme of which was "Unification Theology: With Implications for Ecumenism and Social Action." Representatives of the National Council for the Church and Social Action, in conjunction with the IRF, discussed the necessity for churches to involve themselves in a broad range of social projects. In conferences such as the one in the Bahamas, the Unification worldview is discussed, analyzed, and criticized by knowledgeable religious people. Contrary to the mythology of the media, which presents our church as a secret cult whose members lack all critical awareness, our church is one of the few I know that always seeks to discuss its beliefs in the context of other religious traditions. Our graduate Unification Theological Seminary in Barrytown, New York, sponsors additional ecumenical conferences on campus coordinated by the students themselves for their divinity programs. Eighty percent of the faculty are members of faiths other than the Unification Church: There are several Protestant theologians, two Catholic philosophers, a Jewish rabbi, and three Unification professors on the faculty.

The seminary is a model of ecumenicity and the more than a hundred students there are of an international and intercultural mix. We have students from Europe, Asia, and Latin America, and Africa, as well as from the United States. Although the seminary was established as recently as 1975, we can see Reverend Moon's commitment to higher education in even the earliest days of our church's growth in America.

There have already been several hundred graduates of the seminary, a good percentage of whom have gone on, with the full support of our church, to study for doctorates at prominent graduate schools in the country. Dr. Tyler Hendricks, a man my wife and I knew from our California church, just received his Ph.D. from Vanderbilt University after completing his work at the Unification Theological Seminary. We have other Ph.D. students at Harvard, Yale, Columbia, Emory, Chicago, Vanderbilt, Claremont, Catholic University, and many other schools.

The Unification Theological Seminary also publishes numerous books in conjunction with conferences and dialogues. Several recent titles include: *Hermaneutics and Horizon: the Shape of the Future*, edited by Professor Frank K. Flinn; *The Social Impact of New Religious Movements*, edited by Professor Bryan Wilson; and *Ten Theologians Respond to the Unification Church*, edited by Professor Herbert Richardson.

In these books there is no propaganda, no self-serving essays on behalf of the Unification Church. The eminent theologians whose essays are contained in them are not reluctant to write penetrating criticisms of every aspect of the Unification movement.

Reverend Moon also inspired and initially supported the formation of the Global Congress of the World's Religions. (GCWR).For the past several years preliminary meetings of The Global Congress have been held in San Francisco, Boston, and Los Angeles. The "Notes of the Charter" of the GCWR sets forth the purpose of the organization:

The Global Congress of the World's Religions is a voluntary association of concerned persons from the broad spectrum of all the world's many religions and spiritual perspectives. It was founded in 1980 to become the ongoing forum where representatives from the plurality of human religious experience could communicate with one another, learn about and from one another, and provide means whereby the deepest and highest motivations of both traditionally religious and other persons of spiritual conviction could be creatively and constructively focused for the good of all.

As a complement to his work with professors, scientists, and ministers, Reverend Moon has inspired a university student ministry called the Collegiate Association for the Research of Principles. (CARP) CARP membership is open to all students regardless of their religious background, and local CARP chapters can be found at most major universities. CARP seeks to revitalize the spirit of Judeo-Christian values on campuses and to research a God-centered ideology in order to propose a healthy and intelligent alternative to exclusively materialistic and worldly values. CARP encourages dedication and service to the nation's college communities and seeks to demonstrate that traditional religious standards of morality are still healthy ideals for today's young people.

The performing arts are also very much a part of Reverend Moon's vision for a God-centered world, and thus a number of groups have been established to express the ideals of harmony, unity, and beauty through music, dance, and drama. The church sponsors a wide variety of cultural and artistic groups: the New Hope Singers International, the Korean Folk Ballet, the Go World Brass Band, and several rock and popular music groups. We have also purchased the former Manhattan Opera House in New York City as a showcase for the performing arts and religious activities.

Also dedicated to the performing arts is the Little Angels School, which was founded by Reverend Moon in Seoul, South Korea several years ago. It has an enrollment of 3,600 students, with training from kindergarten through high school. Students from this school have entered Seoul National University, the nation's most prestigious university, in greater percentages than students from any other high school in the country. The school has been called the "Juilliard of Korea," and the Performing Arts Center, which is an adjunct to it, contains the most beautiful theater in the nation. Plans have been made for establishing a Sun Myung Moon University, and we expect that this will be opened in the near future.

Ocean Church is one of the more unique projects of the Unification movement. The ocean, symbolic of a prosperous life, has always been a helpmate of man. Ocean Church sees the sea as a refreshing place to commune with God and to seek spiritual as well as physical nourishment. Church activities focus on communities whose sustenance and future lies with the seas, while programs emphasize the development of human character, seamanship skills, and the art of fishing. Last summer my two sons spent a week with the Ocean Church project in Gloucester, Massachusetts. During their first day on Cape Cod Bay they were on a boat that caught a 658-pound tuna. You should hear the fish stories they tell around my house about the ones that got away.

When our members first began fishing in Cape Cod, we almost immediately began catching more fish than the seasoned old timers. Rumors began to spread that we had developed a technique for brainwashing fish! Other rumors said that Reverend Moon had taught our members to pour a magic elixir over the boat so that tuna would be drawn to our hooks. After several years now, the secret of success has been revealed: hard work, diligence, study, and a lot of prayer.

When one hears of the numerous projects sponsored by the Unification Church, or supported through its donations, one question invariably pops up: Where does the money come from? The question is usually asked with skepticism, as if to talk about money were to move from the realm of religion into the world of scatology. I have found the public to have an almost universally negative reaction when religion and money are discussed in the same context. The truth is, though, that to carry on the charitable, humanitarian, and educational projects of a religion, one needs not only inspiration, but funds.

The Unification Church acquires its monetary support in much the same way traditional religions have for centuries. The time-honored practice of tithing is encouraged. Contributions are received from individuals and other entities wishing to support the church, while members also participate in fundraising campaigns to solicit contributions from the general public.

Besides the obvious monetary benefits to be gained from fundraising campaigns, the church encourages its members to undertake this activity for a deeper reason. The experience to be gained in dealing with many different people is an invaluable part of character development. Furthermore, church teachings emphasize that money, as all things, should be used unselfishly for the betterment of all. The training received in fundraising campaigns is, therefore, invaluable as a religious and educational tool.

Some members of the church support themselves by operating restaurants, health food stores, and fish markets. Others are doctors, lawyers, and teachers. As with members of any religion, we must live and work in the world if we are to serve Heaven. It seems to me the ultimate absurdity for our church to be condemned for being involved in business, or accused of having a business "front," when our members and our church merely perform activities that are necessary for life and growth.

It is true that Reverend Moon is the inspiration behind some highly visible businesses such as newspapers, but even in the realm of newspapers there are precedents like the *Christian Science Monitor* and the *Deseret News,* which were originally inspired by religious vision. In an age of sensationalist media which often pander to the basest sensibility, Reverend Moon had the vision of creating responsible, ethical media. The core of his vision was of course spiritual, but spiritual ideals must be realized in practical ways.

The Washington Times, founded in 1982, became one of the nation's most prestigious newspapers within its first year of publication. The Unification Church exercises no form of editorial or operational control over this conservative, secular newspaper. *Noticias del Mundo* in New York is fast becoming the largest Spanish language daily newspaper in circulation. Reverend Moon has also inspired *The New York Tribune*, another daily newspaper in New York, and *The Harlem Weekly*, as well as a Korean-language weekly. He has founded newspapers in Asia, Latin America, and Europe. All of these media activities inspired by Reverend Moon's vision are funded by tax-paying business enterprises developed by associates of the church.

I have described only a few of the numerous activities he has inspired or founded. Although any one of these projects would credit its founder with being an extraordinary person, Reverend Moon has literally generated the ideas for almost one hundred and fifty such projects. Surely, he is a formidable figure in this age, so much so that it is perhaps understandable why he has generated so much controversy.

7 / The Church Under Siege: The Anti-Religious Movement

The activities of the Unification movement have made their impact on almost every area of culture: science, philosophy, religion, media, medicine, social service, etc. As a result of this and of the rapid growth of the movement, there has been an incredible reaction by the larger culture. Where people have not understood what Unificationists were doing, they often assumed the worst. Where Unification activities challenged the status quo, or exacerbated an existing situation, public reaction was often violent. As with the growth of other religious movements in the United States, the new was seen to be strange and threatening.

In 1919 Helen Jackson of Toledo, Ohio, produced a book entitled *Convent Cruelties or My Life in a Convent,* a classic of anti-cult literature. The sub-title of the book, which went through seven editions by 1924, is "a providential delivery from Rome's convent slave years—a sensational experience."[1] The cult under attack is the Roman Catholic Church. In the nineteenth and early twentieth centuries, long before anyone ever heard of a Moonie or Krishna, there was a concerted "anti-cult" movement by Protestants and secularists against Catholics. Honestly, if you substitute the word "Moonie" for "Catholic" in this book and others like it, it could be pushed today as part of the anti-cult crusade.

Actually, whenever a religious movement appears to be vital, there usually follows an anti-religious reaction that seeks to denigrate and dehumanize it. Roman writers, for example, made comments like the following about the early Christians:

"There is a group, hated for their abominations, called Christians. . . ." (Tacitus)

"The Christians are a class of men given to a new and wicked superstition." (Suetonius)

"They are like frogs holding a symposium around a swamp. . . ." (Celsius)

Bamber Gascoigne, in his history entitled *The Christians,* writes of how:

> ...the early Christians met in secret for their communal meal, and soon it gave rise to all sorts of rumors. They called it an *agape,* or love feast, from a Greek word meaning brotherly love. Love feast! There was talk in no time of sexual orgies in dark and secret places. And word also got around of the Christians eating the flesh and blood of some leader of theirs. Cannibalism now![2]

History repeats itself. In Boston in 1834, an angry mob of some thousand men burned an Ursuline Catholic nunnery. It was the result of anti-Catholic feeling running high in America at that time. In 1844 the Mormon prophet, Joseph Smith, lost his life at the hands of a mob in Carthage, Illinois. In 1981 a Unification Church building in upstate New York was burned to the ground after a burning cross was placed on the

125

front lawn.

There is an increasing network of people involved in a campaign to restrict religious liberty, and they have special designs to stamp out new religious faiths that surface in America. This anti-religious movement is composed basically of five major groups: parents of members of new faiths; Christian heresy hunters; Jewish anti-conversionists; mental health experts who abridge religious freedom; and sensationalist media.

Parents of Members

Throughout history, parents have been shocked when their son or daughter chose a way of life different from their own. Published in 1837 was a book entitled *The Experience of Several Eminent Methodist Preachers; With an Account of Their Call to and Success in the Ministry.*[3] The following is an account of the consternation of one preacher's family after their son became involved with the Methodists.

> In the latter end of June I went to Otley to hear a Methodist preach, when I was more surprised than ever. The serious, devout behavior of the people struck me with a kind of religious awe. The singing greatly delighted me, and the sermon was much blessed to my soul. They suffered me to stay in the society meeting, for which I had great cause to bless God. I returned home full of good resolutions; but little thought I of what trials were coming upon me. I thought certainly none who love me can be offended at my seeking salvation of my soul; but I soon found my mistake. For those who

had formerly been my greatest friends now became my open enemies. All my relations were exceedingly offended, and threatened me much if I would not leave this way. My uncle, in particular, who before promised to be kind to me, now resolved to leave me nothing, which resolution he made good. My father and mother were exceedingly troubled, supposing me to be totally ruined; and my brothers and sisters were of the same mind. My father threatened many times to turn me out of doors, and entirely disown me; but the love he had for me (I being his eldest son) moved him to use every means he could think of to prevail on me to forsake this despised people, whom he hated above all others. He mourned to see me 'run willfully to my own ruin.' My mother also frequently wept much on my account.[4]

How remarkably similar is the response of some families today when religion affects one of its members.

Today, if a parent is unhappy about his grown child's involvement in a religious movement, he can vent his anger by using a most potent weapon: the media. From *The New York Times* to the *National Enquirer*, the media has been only too happy to be the willing listeners to emotionally distressed parents. Fear and emotion are then reported as fact stranger than fiction: "How Family Smashed a Cult's Shackles and Saved a Child."

A few parents have conjured up bizarre images of religious "cults" and then declared war on them. Although the word "cult" is originally a neutral word signifying a small group, it has taken on irrational and monstrous connotations. Thus anyone belonging to such a group is automatically defined as a hideous monster who, once labeled, need no longer be dealt with as a human being.

In every experience I have had with families hostile to our church, I could perceive that serious problems plagued that family long before anyone ever became involved in our church. Families in America have been crumbling during the last fifty years. Hundreds of books have been written offering numerous explanations for this. When Reverend Moon entered the American scene in 1972 and spoke of the God-centered, nuclear family as the hope of a peaceful, ethical world, he attracted numerous followers. Ironically, he was then accused of breaking up families.

The fact is that only a small number of families have been hostile to us, but they have employed the mass media in a spectacular way. (The media, of course, is unexcited by the overwhelming number of families who are positive about or supportive of our church.) Two years ago, for example, a young lady in her late twenties joined the Collegiate Association for the Research of Principles in California. She had been traveling in Europe for several years prior to joining CARP and had not been back to see her family in New Zealand all during that time.

Shortly after she joined CARP, her parents in New Zealand were informed by a "friend" that she had been "captured" by the Moonies. Her mother and sister quickly flew to California and contacted the local Unification Church center and demanded that they turn over their daughter. When she visited with her family, she was told that she had lost her mind and should immediately go with them to see a special counselor working with deprogrammers. She expressed concern for her family's distress and offered to go with them to see the priest at the Berkeley Newman Center. They would have none of it.

She then left for a CARP activity in New York. Her mother and sister, meanwhile, held press conferences and went to every newspaper, television, and radio station in the San Francisco Bay area. Their relative, they said, was being held in San Francisco against her will by the Unification Church, a story dutifully reported by the media just as it was told to them. Since the sister was a reporter herself, her family gained extra sympathy from the news media.

In response to the media blitz in San Francisco, the young woman held a press conference in New York and explained what nonsense was going on. Since San Francisco does not quite recognize or acknowledge New York culture, the horror stories in the Bay area continued. The family escalated their activities. They went to court and persuaded a judge that he should begin contempt proceedings against me, the president of the Unification Church, for holding the woman against her will. (I knew nothing of the situation, as I happened to be in Korea at the time.) The beginning of contempt proceedings means virtually nothing unless one can prove there is a crime, which of course there was not in this case.

Enter the international media. "President of Unification Church of America held in contempt over kidnapping girl." When I returned to the United States

my friends asked when I was going to jail. Several professor friends of mine had read the story in the *International Herald Tribune* in Cairo, Egypt. When we met
upon their return to the United States, they wanted to
know when I had gotten out of jail! Of course nothing
happened except in the media.

A handful of hostile parents have caused literally
thousands of negative articles to be written, all of which
have almost no substance if read objectively. One
wealthy woman in Marin County, California, prides
herself on being the source of more bad press against
the church than anyone else. Like the true religious
zealot, she has staked out a war-room in her home, as
she explained to the *San Francisco Chronicle,* in which she
devotes a great deal of her time, influence, and money
to discrediting the Unification Church. She is only too
happy to give interviews to people who are hostile to us.
She never mentions the drugs, alcohol abuse, or sexual
promiscuity that filled her son's life before he became a
member of the church. Rather, she talks about how
frightened she became when he started praying in the
morning, when he got a job, and when he started act-
ing like a responsible citizen.

The fact is that the majority of relatives of current
members of our church are at the very least accepting,
and often supportive, of the Unification Church. This
has become more and more the case as members have
married and now begun parenting their own families.

Christian Heresy Hunters

Christian heresy hunting must be viewed within the
larger context of the American religious community. It

is not uncommon, and in fact considered perfectly natural, for the clergy of one faith to feel threatened by a member of their congregation becoming an adherent of another faith. It is frequent for there to be fierce competition, and sometimes even back-biting, among well-established Christian denominations. Newer religions are merely easier targets for attack, since they have not yet gained the legitimacy of the more established groups.

Some ministers and their church members have "rescued" their children from the Unification Church and other new religions, either by force or by trying to discredit the new religions. Other ministers have formed groups to "inform the public and battle the menace of the cults." Needless to say, the information is less than unbiased. Several ministers appear to be on individual crusades against the new religions. Anti-cult educational programs are offered at Christian churches nationwide with a traveling band of "experts" who are always ready to whip up a little hysteria.

A few Catholic priests have also been involved in campaigns against the new religions. One prominent priest in New York City has said, "The only clean break [with the cult]. . . is deprogramming." My only personal experience with this priest was when I was invited to appear with him on a New York City television show. When I arrived at the studio, I learned that he would appear on the same show, but not at the same time. I was to wait in the green room and could watch him on TV, then go on the set for my own appearance. The good father insisted that I remain in a different room until he left the building. His remarks, needless to say, were filled with misunderstanding, ignorance and hostility toward the Unification Church. At least I could appear on the show; I don't usually get such opportunities to respond.

The central argument against us is that we attract people in their twenties who are at a vulnerable point in their lives, and that they can therefore be unfairly influenced by us. The reality is that most people are born into their religious faith, are educated or indoctrinated from the earliest age, and never consciously choose one religion over another. My rabbi, when I was thirteen years old, did not offer me a clear choice between Baptist theology, Islamic theology, or Jewish theology. It was assumed that I would be faithful to Jewish theology or I would go to hell. Only in relationship to choosing a different religion must one make a painful, thoughtful, and difficult choice. Young people are usually more courageous and flexible about religious conversion than older people. Habit makes cowards of us all.

Jewish Anti-Conversionists

It is truly unfortunate that some of the bitterest enemies of the Unification Church are members of the Jewish faith. In a statement about the Unification movement published in January 1976, Reverend Moon said: "We consider ourselves to be the younger brother to our Jewish and Christian brethren, all of whom are children of our Heavenly Father. We regard it as our duty to respect and serve Judaism and Christianity by promoting love and unity among all the children of God." Such words of friendship followed three years of Jewish opposition, which still continues.

These opponents form basically three groups: already established Jewish groups, which attack new religions as part of their defense of Judaism; new groups founded by 'anti-cult' rabbis; and lone Jewish crusaders.

B'nai B'rith, "the oldest and largest Jewish service organization in the world," is strongly opposed to the new religions. One of its documents seeks to institute "a national program designed to educate adults and youth as to the menace the cults present, and to speak out wherever and whenever necessary until the threat of these cults is eliminated." B'nai B'rith has supported a bill in Maryland to investigate "cult phenomenon" and wrote letters to former Gov. Hugh Carey of New York in 1980 endorsing the signing of the Lasher Conservatorship Bill, which would have empowered the government to certify members of new religions as "mentally incompetent," and allow parents to take custody of them. Imagine the outcry if such a bill were sponsored against the Jews.

The National Council of Young Israel has also come out strongly against new religions, particularly the Unification Church. They have issued a proclamation: "This is a warning to parents and children. The cults—Moonies, Hare Krishna, Children of God, and the missionary organizations are making inroads in all circles to lure our children to conversion. . . . This is our last stand in a war declared on our very existence as Jews." Jewish opposition to the cults is part of a larger scheme of Jewish opposition to *all* Christian (or other evangelical) outreach. Unfortunately, this is a problem that will take many years of Jewish-Christian dialogue

133

to resolve, for "bearing witness to the word" is an essential component to the Christian faith. Again, in this context, the new religions are merely the easiest targets or weakest links, in a much larger chain being attacked by the Jewish community.

Rabbi Maurice Davis seems to be the originator of the anti-religious movement in Judaism. In early 1974 he began writing articles against the Unification Church and started deprogramming its members. At that time he wrote: "I know them [Unification Church members] for what they are, and I am their enemy. . . . I doubt that the group will be in existence in 1980." In 1975 he helped to establish "Citizens Engaged in Reuniting Families" (CERF). Up to the present he has remained an integral part of the anti-Unification Church movement. Rather than look at why young people are not attracted to his own synagogue, Rabbi Davis has found an enemy to attack.

He shows nothing but disgust for the new religions, and describes members of such religions as prisoners. In my office I have a pile of hate literature published in the Jewish press against the new religions. The articles number in the hundreds. How tragic for the victim of so much religious bigotry to now seek to execute another religious group.

Mental Health Experts Who Abridge Religious Freedom

During the past five or ten years, some mental health experts have begun to decide which religions are proper for people to follow. Chief in this movement are Flo Conway and Jim Siegelman, whose "findings" have been broadcast through the sensationalist media. Conway and Siegelman became interested in cults in 1974 when they researched certain groups for *Harper's* magazine, where they were managing editor and writer/editor respectively. After six years of research they came to the conclusion that the only successful way to break away from a cult is through the controversial technique known as deprogramming. Their book *Snapping: America's Epidemic of Sudden Personality Change* presents analyses of religious experience from the viewpoint of atheistic materialism. Their final conclusion is: "Contrary to popular opinion, our exploration has confirmed for us that there is really nothing *human* inside human beings. It's all biology, chemistry and machinery."[5]

Their second book, which again attempts to discredit religion, is *Holy Terror* (1981), an attack on the fundamentalist evangelical Christian movement. Conway and Siegelman claim that this is the next lunatic fringe group in line after the new religions. Many who were perhaps impressed with their first book now have a keener insight into this team's real motives.

Dr. John Clark is the executive director of the Center on Destructive Cultism, an organization located in Boston and sponsored by the American Family Foundation (AFF). He has reportedly stated that Catholicism was a cult until it grew larger, and that certain monks might still be under mind control. If psychiatry has the power to determine mental illness based on religious beliefs, its treatment could conceivably include such infamous psychiatric techniques as electro-shock therapy, lobotomy, sleep deprivation, and forced drugging, with or without the person's informed consent. In a recent paper published by the Center on Destructive

Cultism ("Destructive Cult Conversions: Theory, Research and Treatment") deprogramming is described as a "sometimes forced reawakening of the convert's old personality," and is described as one of the possible treatments for members of new religions.

"What Dr. Clark...[says]," writes Dr. Lee Coleman, a California psychiatrist who specializes in abuses within the mental health profession, is "that the act of joining an unpopular religion was *in itself* a sign of mental illness." In many cases judges accepted such ideas and granted conservatorships of members of new religions, who were then turned over to parents, psychiatrists, and deprogrammers. "Often the person for whom a conservatorship was requested was not even told such a hearing was taking place. The fact that in many cases the psychiatrists or psychologist had never seen the person, and was basing his professional opinion strictly on information received from the parents, seemed to make no difference to the judges."[6]

Dr. Margaret Singer is a clinical psychologist, a member in good standing of what might be called the American psychology establishment. She has been called as an expert to give evidence before courts. In the past her work has centered on brainwashing techniques used by communists against American POWs in Korea. She is also interested in the new churches and has provided psychological guidance for former members of new religions. She considers herself, and is considered by many, an authority on the new religions and their real or alleged malpractices. Her work, unfortunately, suffers from a variety of disabilities. These include a lack of historical perspective, inadequate knowledge of the comparative theology necessary for a researcher in the field of religion, an apparent failure to grasp the varieties of religious motivation, a seeming unwillingness to consider adherence to an unorthodox religion as a legitimate form of behavior guaranteed under the Constitution, and a remarkable propensity for drawing sweeping conclusions from inadequate evidence.

Her grotesque caricatures of life in a religious movement border on the absurd, yet they have been accepted and repeated over and over again by the general public:

> From the time prospects are invited to the cult's domicile, they are caught up in a round of long, repetitive lectures couched in hypnotic metaphors and exalted ideas....Several groups send their members to bed wearing headsets that pipe sermons into their ears as they sleep. That's after hours of listening to tapes of the leader's exhortations while awake.[7]

To Dr. Singer, everyone in this religious world is a mindless robot who must be saved by the new priest with the new religious theology. Dr. Singer becomes the high priestess of the new psychology. She has her own esoteric knowledge, she is very clear about the evil satans to be destroyed, and she is on a crusade to spread her gospel. Her fees for a court appearance, I am told, are $1,000 a day.

Dr. Singer cannot emancipate herself from her own secular assumptions. As she sees it, religion must not challenge the compartmentalization of life into the separate religious and social spheres. Total religious commitment of the kind once demanded by Jesus and Mohammed would certainly appear to her a deviant form of activity. Such commitment is explicable to her only in terms of artful manipulation by mind-benders. The use of coercion for the purpose of restoring the believer to his or her original state of mind makes Dr. Singer all too tolerant of deprogrammers.

The use or abuse of psychiatry to establish norms of behavior is not unfamiliar to the rulers of the Soviet Union. Political dissidents are labeled as mentally incompetent and confined to hospitals for treatment. For, obviously, one must be somewhat abnormal not to appreciate the blessings of Soviet Russia. In logic of the same manner, if one does not embrace the value-free norm of contemporary American culture, there is cause for alarm.

The Sensationalist Media

The media have been referred to as the fourth branch of government. When given the choice between a story about a boy scout who helps ladies as opposed to one who mugs them, the choice will be the more sensational one every time, making the bad press given the Unification Church understandable.

Publications have made a fetish of words like cult, brainwash, slavery, victim. "Cultism Is Emotional Slavery" reads one headline in the *San Francisco Chronicle*.[8] "Moonie 'Brainwash' Charged" reads a second *Chronicle* article.[9] Since San Francisco was the home of Jim Jones's People's Temple, any unorthodox religion (in the eyes of the *Chronicle*) becomes fair game for sensational coverage. The *Chronicle,* like most other newspapers, overlooks the fact that Jones's congregation was part of a mainline denomination, not even of a small sect.

"Moon Accused of Plotting to Rule World" reads a headline in the *Modesto Bee,* a California newspaper that picked up a UPI story.[10] The article describes, in tones suggesting clandestine evil, the growth of the international Unification movement. "Reverend Moon Wants You" was once the lead story of the *Reader,* San Diego's weekly magazine.[11] Finally, the media have had a field day making word games with Reverend Moon's name. "The Dark Side of Moon"[12] is a title that has been repeated many times in the last ten years.

Remembering *Convent Cruelties* of 1919, we get a better perspective on the media's need for a scapegoat. In June 1880, the newspaper *The Protestant Vindicator* published the preamble of an anti-Catholic society:

> . . . whereas, the influence of Romanism is rapidly extending throughout this Republic, endangering the peace and freedom of our country—therefore, being anxious to preserve the ascendancy of 'pure religion' and to maintain and perpetuate the genuine truths of Protestantism unadulterated, with devout confidence and the sanction of the great head of the Church to aid our efforts in withstanding the 'power in great authority of the beast and the strong delusion of the False Prophet,' we do hereby agree to be governed by the following constitution.

139

Simply change a few of the phrases in the previous statement and you have many people's description of the Unification Church, or any of the other new religions. In the introduction to his book *New Religions and Mental Health,* Dr. Herbert Richardson draws succinct parallels between the anti-Catholic and anti-Semitic propaganda of the nineteenth and early twentieth centuries, and the anti-cult propaganda of the later twentieth century. *(See chart page 142.)*

The stories about the Unification Church are part of the genre of anti-religious literature that Professor Harvey Cox describes in his article "Myths Sanctioning Religious Persecution."[13] Essentially, these false myths purport to describe the religious group in the following manner: The group will deceive you ("heavenly deception"); it is dominated by a foreign influence (the Pope or the KCIA); the leader is a charlatan; and the group uses the technique of "the evil eye" to capture the mind and soul of its converts. The stereo types continue *ad nauseum.*

Jesus was perhaps the most controversial figure of human history. While he was alive he received accusations from Romans and Jews, rich and poor, pious and proud. There was, and continues to be, a great deal of accusation against his life and work. So, too, is there against anyone who seeks to do God's work in any large way.

Finally, one might ask: What about the ex-member of a faith who makes the same accusations as those who know nothing of the group? The *only* ex-members I know who have made public accusations against the Unification Church were those who were violently kidnapped, locked up, and coerced into recanting their beliefs. This criminal activity of deprogramming or "faithbreaking" has as its central purpose the destruction of a church member's belief in the church itself, its leaders, and practices. As love turns quickly to hate, a trusting believer can become a cynical bigot. How? Let us analyze the process.

Anti-Catholicism	Anti-Semitism	Anti-Cultism
The Pope is seeking to take over the world.	The Jews are seeking to take over the world. (The Protocols of the Elders of Zion)	Moon is seeking to take over the world.
Catholicism is not a true religion, but a political system.	Judaism is not a religion, but a political system.	The Unification Church is not a church, but a political front group.
Catholics aren't loyal Americans, but are really loyal to Rome, a foreign power.	Jews aren't loyal Americans, but are really loyal to Israel.	Moon teaches Americans to fight for Korea.
The Catholic Church exploits the poor in order to build rich churches and buy land.	Jews are really only after money.	Moon claims to be a prophet, but is really only after profit.
The priests enslave the minds of young people, inculcating irrational superstition.	Judaism is a legalistic, tribalistic system, ritualistic and anti-rational.	Moon brainwashes his converts.

142

Catholics control their young people's lives by teaching that sex is evil.	Jews control their young people's lives by making them feel guilty about marrying a non-Jew	Moon controls young people's lives by making them remain chaste and then arranging their marriages.
Catholics justify lying by "mental reservation."	Jews always lie.	Moonies don't tell the truth, but practice "heavenly deception."
Catholics entice children, while too young to decide for themselves, to become nuns and priests.	Jews kidnap gentile children for vile purposes.	Moon entices the young to leave their families.
Catholics are swarthy (Latin) and have too many children.	Jews have crooked noses and are verminous.	Moonies have glazed eyes and are undernourished.

From Herbert Richardson, ed., *New Religions and Mental Health* (New York and Toronto: the Edwin Mellen Press, 1980) p. xxvii, reprinted by permission.

8 / "Deprogramming": Abduction, Kidnapping, and Faithbreaking

The most serious threat of the anti-religious movement to both civil and religious liberty is the criminal activity of deprogramming. The word "deprogram," like cult, is loaded jargon used by those hostile to a particular religion. If you do not like another's beliefs, you claim they have been programmed or brainwashed. You may then feel responsible for de-programming or un-washing the minds of such unfortunate people. Since you do not believe they can think straight, you cannot use logic, discussion, or information to change their beliefs. What is necessary is to kidnap them and lock them up in a controlled environment where they can be forced to see another point of view. You continue the forced imprisonment, intimidation, and harassment until they change and you can break their faith. Such is the nature of deprogramming.

The public is generally unaware that this is a crime whose perpetrators have victimized thousands of people of virtually every religious group in America. Ironically, the public believes that it is the religious groups that imprison members and hold them against their will. Further, the public believes that when deprogramming occurs, it is only in the context of cults, and thus is to be tolerated. The real story of this violent abuse of religious liberty has yet to be told.

Ted Patrick, considered to be the "father" of the modern deprogramming movement, has set himself up as a specialist with a mission to destroy cults and pseudo-religions. Although his background, as with almost all deprogrammers, includes only a high school education, he has been quoted as an authority on new religions in magazines like *Playboy,* and has been praised for his book *Let Our Children Go*. He lumps together most religions he does not like and calls them "Manson-like," claiming that the central power exerted by them is the use of mind control. In *Let Our Children Go* he describes his exploits in heroic, crusader-like terms, admitting to practicing the very things he claims to see in the new religions: physical violence, imprisonment, harassment of individuals.

In a March 1979 *Playboy* interview Patrick says:

> What I do is not kidnapping. What I do is rescuing. When I deprogram a person, he has already been unlawfully imprisoned. His mind has been unlawfully imprisoned by a cult. . . . The so-called experts on brainwashing make me glad I didn't go to college. Those people don't realize you don't have to use torture any more. It's all done with love and kindness—and deception. . . . TM is one of the damaging forms of meditation. It's also one of the biggest cults in the nation. . . . When I deprogram someone, I work with a security team. We have somebody accompany the person to the bathroom. Then, at night, one person sleeps

across from him and another sleeps in front of the door. . . . Hell, Jimmy Carter's sister is one of the biggest cult leaders in the nation. Ruth Stapleton uses all the same techniques they do. She's nothing but a cult leader. . . . she programs people. I've seen members do it in meetings, and she's got a mailing list like you wouldn't believe. I also have reason to think she's using the same techniques on members of the government. I saw one Cabinet member on TV talking about how he was born again through Ruth Carter Stapleton. He looked just like a Moonie, glazed eyes, the works. . . . (pp. 53, 58, 77, 120)[1]

How does Ted Patrick gently persuade someone to join him in dialogue? He gives us a clear picture in his book *Let Our Children Go*. Wes, a member of a new religious group, has been surrounded by Patrick and some of his goons:

Wes had taken up a position facing the car, with his hands on the roof and his legs spreadeagled. There was no way to get him inside while he was braced like that. I had to make a quick decision. I reached down between Wes's legs, grabbed him by the crotch and squeezed—hard. He let out a howl, and doubled up, grabbing for his groin with both hands. Then I hit, shoving him head first into the back of the car and piling in on top of him.[2]

What kind of logic and moral persuasion does Patrick use in his discussion with the captive? "Moon is a pimp. He's a pimp, that's all, and you're nothing but a

1. *"Playboy* Interview with Ted Patrick," March 1979, pp. 53, 58, 77, 120, Copyright © 1979 by *Playboy*.

male prostitute. You've given yourself to him body and soul, and you go out in the streets and sell yourself and bring the money back to him."[3]

The pattern of kidnapping, forced imprisonment, and intimidation is the same for all those engaged in the faithbreaking process. There are, however, various methods by which kidnappers will attempt to break the religious faith of his victim. If the victim is moved by the tears of a former girlfriend or boyfriend, then extended conversations between the two, with or without seduction, will follow. Distraught parents are brought into the room to induce guilt. "How can your religious group be so pure if you have caused us such pain?" Tapes of former members who had their faith broken are then played to induce the same breaking in the current captive. Selective information is offered as proof that the leaders are frauds and only out for their self-interest.

When a member of our church is kidnapped by Galen Kelly, for example, who, like the other kidnappers, charges many thousands of dollars per head, he introduces his standard manual of so-called "information" to discredit church leaders. He will drag out charges about Reverend Moon that the victim has never before seen. When confronted by captors and kidnappers with distortions, untruths, and half-truths, the victim is made to believe that he or she has been following a charlatan. Of course, the captive is never given a chance to call church officials for their explanations of the material or given access to means to challenge his captors.

A favorite ploy of kidnappers is to try to discredit me because of volunteer work I did at Lewisburg Penitentiary in Pennsylvania. In 1967-68, when I was a professor at Lycoming College in Pennsylvania, a friend of mine and I established an educational program for convicts at Lewisburg. I have sometimes mentioned this experience over the years as one that awakened me to the need for profound structural change in our society. When a victim is held captive he is shown a letter by the warden of the penitentiary to the effect that he never knew me and I never "worked" at Lewisburg. I am not sure what warden has written this letter, but I know of members whose faith has been shaken by this simple deception of kidnappers. One bit of disinformation is piled upon another.

Abduction and restraint, sleep deprivation, guilt inducement, violence, verbal abuse, harassment, and outright deception are all means used to draw someone away from religious commitment. Michael K., a current member of the Unification Church, tells how in June 1976, while shopping with his mother in New York City, he was tackled from behind by several men, including Galen Kelly, and pushed into the back of a van. He was held down by four men, one holding each leg and another his arm. Galen Kelly sat on his chest and held his hand over his mouth to prevent him from shouting for assistance. His arm was twisted, causing considerable pain, and his mouth so tightly gagged he feared he would suffocate. Michael was kidnapped several times in a similar manner. Each time he escaped and continued to trust and seek a good relationship with his family, yet he maintained his commitment to his religious ideals.

A new institution has been built up by the

faithbreakers, a kind of spiritual brothel, a center where relatives pay kidnappers to exercise the pleasure of their ways upon their captives. The Freedom of Thought Foundation in Tuscon, Arizona, was one such house of pleasure. When Barbara Underwood's parents took out a secret conservatorship order on her in California, claiming that she had become mentally incompetent since joining the Unification Church, she was taken for treatment to the lonely house in Tucson.

With bars on the windows and guard dogs prowling the isolated desert landscape surrounding the house, Barbara was given the "freedom" to think "objectively" about her life of faith. Gary Scharff, the scholar in residence, eventually gave her a passing mark as she lost her faith. She was then rushed to the local newspaper to tell how she had discovered the evils of her former ways. Barbara and Gary have now been rushing to the media and into the arms of potential clients for several years.

What happened to the Reverend Walter Taylor, an Old Catholic priest, when he was abducted from a monastery in Oklahoma City and brought to Akron, Ohio?

My monastic clothes were ripped off me while four persons held me down. My...crucifix was taken away from me. I was harassed for thirteen hours or more per day about my religious beliefs by various persons working in shifts. I was kept awake and not permitted to sleep on various occasions when I wanted to sleep....I was threatened with commitment to a mental institution if I did not cooperate and renounce my religion. . . .[4]

The priest said that Phoenix attorney Wayne Howard and a deprogrammer named Gary Scharff were present part of the time. Howard and a Tucson attorney, Michael E. Trauscht, and a clinical psychologist from Tucson, Kevin M. Gilmartin, cooperate in deprogramming efforts from Arizona.

Who are some of the kidnapping victims? Debbie Dudgeon, a practicing member of the Roman Catholic faith; Peter Willis, a member of the Episcopal Church of the Redeemer; Susan Wirth, a thirty-five-year-old woman involved with liberal politics in San Francisco; Stephanie Reithmiller, a computer operator, who had a female roommate that her parents did not like. The list of victims, and the reasons for their kidnappings is almost endless. And yet one hears almost nothing except, "Oh, it's just one of those cult members." That is usually the attitude of the local police, the FBI, and other law enforcement officials when they are asked to prevent an or interfere in an abduction. Often, they will actively aid the kidnappers. "Oh, it's only a family affair." Of course, the multimillion-dollar aspect of this kidnapping racket is overlooked.

The professionals and groups who have studied the deprogramming-faithbreaking criminal activity always condemn it. Only those few who benefit financially or who are opposed to freedom for the beliefs of others seek to justify it. They speak of the process as counseling, although they neglect to mention the "expert" qualifications of Ted Patrick, Galen Kelly, Joe Alexander and their like.

Deprogramming has been denounced by religious bodies, constitutional experts, civil libertarians and mental health authorities:

NATIONAL COUNCIL OF CHURCHES
The Governing Board of the National Council of Churches believes that religious liberty is one of the most precious rights of humankind, which is grossly violated by forcible abduction and protracted efforts to change a person's religious commitments by duress. Kidnapping for ransom is heinous indeed, but kidnapping to compel religious deconversion is equally criminal. It violates not only the letter and spirit of state and federal statutes but the world standard of the Universal Declaration of Human Rights.

AMERICAN CIVIL LIBERTIES UNION
The current epidemic of 'deprogramming' of religious followers by professionals who blithely violate the laws of the land while the authorities 'look the other way' is ominous and...[is] an early warning sign for the American people. This is a tricky business, and the freedom of an individual to choose his own religion and even his own lifestyle is at stake.

RELIGIOUS LIBERTARIANS

Dean Kelley, the Director for Religious Liberty for

the National Council of Churches:
It should be prosecuted, not just as any other kidnapping undertaken for mercenary motives should be, but even more vigorously, since it strikes at the most precious and vulnerable portion of the victim's life, religious convictions and commitments.

Dr. James Penton, Professor of History at the University of Lethbridge, and Vice-President of Canadians for the Protection of Religious Liberty:
Deprogramming is a violation of human rights. If an adult makes a choice—never mind whether that choice is wise or not, self-directed or not—the choice should be respected. Deprogrammers who literally snatch people off the street and then subject them to intensive 'reprogramming,' are breaking laws.

MENTAL HEALTH EXPERTS

Lee Coleman, MD, Psychiatrist in Berkeley, California:
Deprogramming, however, is unmistakably an example of the end justifying the means. Crimes (kidnapping and false imprisonment) are committed and then justified in order to rescue the brainwashed convert. I maintain that persons engaging in or condoning such criminal behavior have no solid moral platform on which to make their allegations against new religious movements. They must first renounce their own vigilante tactics.

Annual Convention of the New England Psychological Association at Clark University Worchester, Massachusetts, November 12-13, 1977:
We the undersigned members of the professional psychological community protest the use of coercive 'deprogramming,' disguised as psychological therapy, to force adult individuals to renounce their religious beliefs and affiliations. We regard such tactics as a serious threat to civil liberty in America.

SOCIOLOGISTS

David G. Bromley and *Anson D. Shupe, Jr.* Associate Professor and Chairman of the Department of Sociology, University of Hartford, Connecticut, and Associate Professor of Sociology, University of Texas, respectively:
Deprogrammers are like the American colonials who persecuted 'witches': A confession, drawn up before the subject was brought in for torturing...based on the judges' fantasies about witchcraft, was signed under duress and then treated as justification for the torture. *In the end, the similarity of ex-members' stories is not the result of similar experiences but rather of artifical and imposed reinterpretations by persons serving their own needs and purposes.* Deprogrammers are self-serving, illegal, and fundamentally immoral. In some cases, despite their protests to the contrary, they have profited handsomely from this practice. [Emphasis added.]

The story of deprogramming has yet to be told to the American public. Members of new religious movements do as many dumb things as members of old religious movements. But, overwhelmingly, they are more sinned against than sinning.

9 / Mistakes in Building the Kingdom

If the anti-religious movement and the criminal activities directed against the Unification Church have served some good, it has allowed us to think more honestly and clearly about the mistakes I and others have made in our zeal to build the Kingdom of God on earth. There have been many mistakes, but none of them malicious, devious, illegal, or intended to defraud, as our detractors charge. Rather, our mistakes are those made in youthful zeal and out of ignorance. Perhaps our mistakes are even understandable and forgivable, since no one has ever offered a course or written a book on how to found and establish a religion. Quite frankly, we had to learn about church-building through on-the-job training, by trial and error. I suspect that other religious pioneers have had the same experience.

Over the past dozen years we have experienced both internal and external difficulties in the building of the Unification Church, some due to our own mistakes and others due to the hostility of others. In 1972, the Unification Church in America was a tiny group of people, less than three hundred in three or four cities. Our numbers have multiplied some one hundred and fifty times in ten years. When I opened my house and three brothers moved in, the Unification Church of America was only a vision, not a reality. Within a year, my home was crowded. As I related earlier, we had to buy a house on Hearst Street, an old fraternity house near Berkeley, to deal with our expanded core membership. We needed buses, and we purchased those. We obtained land in the Boonville area of Northern California. We purchased another house on Regent Street, and then others. Suddenly, an institution, a church, was mushrooming around us.

At first, I simply chucked my teaching check into the pot, while others put in what they made from their jobs. Whenever anything was needed, a bus or a van, we bought it with money from the pot. But as we grew and our needs became larger, we saw the necessity of becoming businesslike and formal. We acquired lawyers and accountants by fits and starts. We had to learn through each new activity.

In fundraising, we had similar experiences. At first when we had a special project, we sold sandwiches out of baskets on the street and never thought about permits. After all, we were students and teachers and knew nothing of such things. Later, when we learned, we made every effort to obtain permits wherever legally needed. Sometimes cities refused us. We went to court and eventually won over a hundred cases to obtain permits. No one publicizes our court victories and the fact that such refusals to grant permits are unconstitutional. Some overzealous members have sometimes fundraised without permits, but we have always tried to correct and guard against such oversights. You cannot always make volunteers do things properly. It is very difficult directing volunteers, and everyone in our church is indeed a volunteer. Our innocence led us to feel that we were the first people ever to build a church. Indeed, we often felt we were the first people to discover God, for this was the first time that we ourselves had felt moved by God's spirit.

Our movement attracted many different kinds of people, some quite mature, some still maturing, and others immature. People with problems before joining the Unification Church retained those problems. People with difficulties with their parents retained those difficulties and often exacerbated them. Indeed, most Unification Church members who have had problems with their families were alienated from home before they joined us. More than this, when secular parents saw their children join a religious group, any religious group, they were incensed. For them, all religion was just a fraud, a waste of time. When Jewish young people joined and their parents heard that we taught something about Jesus, they sometimes went into panic.

In 1979 one prominent, wealthy, Jewish couple from Washington, D.C., heard that their twenty-six-year-old son was attending a Unification seminar in San Francisco. In a rage, they flew out and appeared at the church where they created a mild hysteria, demanding that their son return with them immediately. So the man did indeed leave with them. For years his parents wrote articles for newspapers, magazines, and journals condemning the horrors of the Unification Church. I had met with the young man before he left with them. He told me the sad story of how little love he was able to receive from his parents, and explained the sham of their materialist, decadent lifestyle. In attacking the Unification Church his parents were able to assuage the guilt of a lifetime of failure with their son.

We surely made some mistakes dealing with families, but they were mistakes of omission; we were faced with uncompromising prejudice and misunderstandings. Since we were just beginning, we failed to immediately perceive the need for trained counselors to help our members deal with their complicated family relationships.

The press loved to exploit parental panic and prejudice in the following way: Unification seminars are usually held on weekends at a country retreat. Several hundred participants attend these seminars, which are structured into three one-hour lectures daily, with small group discussions following the larger lecture. Let us say that a parent of a participant suddenly appears at the entrance to the seminar facility and demands to see his son or daughter. (Remember, the average age of a participant would be in the mid- to late-twenties.)

Because the person receiving the parent was often young and inexperienced, and because we were naive and unprepared for the incidents, errors were made. If these disturbed people had been allowed in, they would have disrupted the seminar. If a message were sent for a son or daughter to come out, and that person refused, TV reporters duly reported that this "concentration camp" locked up people against their will. Dozens of such incidents occurred and seriously and unjustifiably blackened our reputation. We experienced a combination of prejudice and malice against us, exploited by unethical sensationalists, compounded by the sometimes less than perfect actions of our inexperienced members.

Our relations with the Jewish community have been

the most painful to me personally. I say this with a heavy heart, since I was raised in the Jewish faith and am proud of my heritage. Perhaps much of this regrettable situation grows out of the great fear of the Jewish community that it will lose its young people. The great place Jesus has in our theology also raises Jewish animosity. But I have made my own mistakes, which, however well-meaning, contributed to this painful problem.

In the early days of our movement in California, I and a dozen others who were raised in the Jewish faith decided to organize a volunteer group to support Jewish organizations. This motivation is not unlike the one that has created the numerous ecumenical activities our church now sponsors, and for which we have gained wide recognition. We didn't stop to ask the Jewish community what they thought of our intentions; we just moved forward. That was our typical and unsophisticated style. We wrote up articles of incorporation for our new group, Judaism in Service to the World, drove to Sacramento, incorporated, and celebrated with a dinner.

Our first event was to raise money for the Jewish Welfare Federation by holding a banquet and hiring the Tel Aviv String Quartet to play. We had a friendly relationship with Ben Swig, a Jewish philanthropist and owner of the Fairmont Hotel. Things looked good until the night of the concert, when pickets appeared at the hotel. "Moonies are trying to undermine the Jewish Community," the picket carriers charged. We had made a big mistake—and all the time we had been trying to do good. We raised about $1,000 and attempted to give it to the Jewish Welfare Federation, but they refused it. Later, we donated it anonymously. I still have the canceled check. This whole affair was a result of naivete. We should first have talked to Jewish community leaders.

We have made mistakes, yet every one to my knowledge was innocent, done out of ignorance and the zeal to do good. This is especially true for our response to the abuse by the media. A typical example involves the episode of the celebrated Boonville fence. Since our Boonville retreat center is a converted sheep ranch there was never a fence to close off the property from the main highway. After NBC did its TV special on the "Moonies" at Boonville in 1975, we experienced an invasion of local curiosity seekers, so we put up a make-shift fence only on the automobile entrance to the property, and placed on it a sign that said "NO TRES-PASSING."

Within a week that ominous-looking sign appeared on the front page of the *San Francisco Chronicle*. Our group was obviously trying to hide something, wrote the author of the article. We were foolish. We should have put up a colorful sign saying "PLEASE RING THE BELL AND WE WILL WELCOME YOU." Today there is no fence and no sign in Boonville, and we are not usually accused of being a secretive group. We pride ourselves on working to establish good relations with our neighbors and with the media. Our progress, however, has come at the expense of much misunderstanding.

Above all, we didn't know how to deal with the media. We had no comprehensive policy. We tried to ignore the papers when they carried only negative stories, but that wasn't the correct thing to do! We didn't realize we needed a public relations person at each church center. Instead, whoever picked up the phone (usually the cook) found himself dealing with journalists. We didn't even have a receptionist at most churches. Disaster! That caused a lot of bad relationships with the public.

Looking back now, we can see the depth and significance of the mistakes we made in ignorance, brashness, and zeal. Parents and reporters who found no responsible person at the Boonville gate, or who got young Charlie in the kitchen on the telephone rather than a receptionist, assumed that the Unification Church was a secret group that hides its members lest they get away. That, of course, is false, and it is only because we did not learn soon enough how eager the press and the antireligious movement are to distort and deceive that the false image of the church was created.

We are not a secret, underhanded group, and yet this perception is still widespread. Part of the reason is that our core members are so mobile. Mail comes for them at one address while they are living at another. Parents may get the idea that mail is intercepted or that their child does not want to answer. It is mobility, not stonewalling, that is involved. When there is hostility, however—and a widespread belief in conspiracy theories abounds—no one thinks of the simple and common-sense explanation.

In actuality, communication in a church like ours, one that is growing very rapidly, is extremely difficult. Our work, like college work, is highly intense. Just as university students often stop writing home because of the pressure of studies and social life, so our members, caught up in newly found responsibilities, projects, and God-consciousness, might often neglect to write home for long periods. This causes problems; however, we always encourage our members to build and improve their family relationships.

The breakdown of communications also arises from one of the more appealing features of our movement: any young person can take on responsibility almost immediately if he or she wishes. As an additional problem, though, this means that we have functioned this past dozen years with often immature leadership. The very exuberance, charisma, and drive of our young leaders has caused many mistakes and brought so many negative reactions to our work. For example, very early after the founding of Project Volunteer we went to Napa County to help migrant workers. One of the other, older social service agencies became upset that "Moonies" were moving into their sphere and involving themselves in aid to the poor. The needs of the migrants were enormous, but the social service agency felt threatened because the Unification Church entered their turf. Perhaps if we were older and wiser we would have sat down and carefully explained what we hoped to do, worked out a plan to eliminate fear and friction, and thus avoided any problems.

That feeling of threat may explain why some in the religious community feel so harshly about the Unification Church. The fact that some Jewish young people became "Moonies" has caused people like Rabbi Maurice Davis to feel that we are stealing the next generation, the Jewish future. We have never had such intentions, of course. And this mistaken notion that we were—and are—a threat to other churches is spread far beyond the synagogue. There are rabbis, priests, pastors, and laity in all churches who feel we are a "satanic lure" to steal their young away. How terrible a misjudgment! Nonetheless, once one gets a bad name, it is difficult to live it down—no matter how unjust that name is.

I offer this account as a sort of confession of my own and my church's shortcomings. Let me deal then with some of the charges made against the Unification Church by the press, the anti-religious movement, and the deprogrammers.

The biggest charge, I feel, is that we practice deception. "Heavenly deception" is a phrase applied to us over and over. Opponents charge that we deceive, by not telling potential recruits—or those from whom we solicit funds—who we are. Many deprogrammed ex-members report that they were members for weeks before they were told about Reverend Moon. The hostile movies about our church all stress this supposed deception. Let me say that insofar as some of our zealous evangelists may have downplayed Reverend Moon in, our earliest contacts in the past, such is now clearly and expressly against our policy and our instructions to members of the church. In fact, after our introductory supper and lecture at evening programs across the country, the members who invite people to come up "to the land" for a seminar say "We will study the teachings of Reverend Moon." Actually, anyone who joins the church signs a membership form that clearly states

"Unification Church." There was and is no desire on our part to deceive. We only want to give others the love of God and the principles needed to understand human life.

The same holds true for charges that our fundraisers deceive by saying they are raising money for drug rehabilitation, Christian youth groups, or other such projects, without identifying the church. It is always wrong for anyone to misrepresent the church, and we try to prevent such occurrences. In the rare instances when they do happen, we correct such practices when they come to our attention. Though misrepresentations may have taken place, these are human and individual shortcomings and not policies of the church, which diligently acts to prevent them. Generally, charges of deception are old ones, going back at least five years. No doubt unfortunate things have happened, but our church is striving to correct them. This has been particularly the case with the abuse of the public's sentimentality by fundraisers going to shopping centers in wheelchairs. There is a kernel of truth in the exaggerated charges made by our opponents. I have handled two such cases since becoming president of the church. I was shocked and took immediate steps to stop such activities.

Actually, two such cases, I refer to in Ohio and Texas, turned out to entail more over-zealousness than deception. Fundraisers are usually on their feet for ten or twelve hours and sometimes develop leg or back problems. Several of our young people were told by a doctor to stay off their feet and rest. However, they wanted to fundraise, so they combined rest for the legs with fundraising by using wheelchairs. I insisted they stop this practice because the public misinterpreted it as deception.

Another charge is that we new religious leaders are rolling in mega-bucks while the membership starves. This is ludicrous. My lifestyle is open to the world. I live in a church-owned house in Berkeley, and it is used as a church meeting place. When in New York, which is 98 percent of the time, my wife and I live in a small one-bedroom apartment in the church's headquarters building. Reverend Moon lives in a large church-owned parsonage in Tarrytown, New York, but is never alone there with his family, for, as I explained, there may be fifty people from all over the world there at any time. Rather than living a life of indolent luxury, both he and I work very hard—extremely hard. Indeed, we work seven days a week until late at night. I don't live in luxury; I draw no salary, and I know Reverend Moon's situation is similar to my own.

Let us, however, use fair standards in evaluating the lifestyle of any leader of a worldwide religious movement. The Pope, the Archbishop of Canterbury, and Billy Graham are all leaders of religious movements. They represent not themselves alone, but millions of followers. Reverend Moon is a public person like each of the other religious leaders, and his lifestyle serves the purpose of his public ministry.

As to members starving, that is absurd. People who say we use protein deprivation on recruits should check the menu at any other church or Boy Scout camp. We never use food weapons on people! Sometimes the very zeal of our leaders can produce a situation upon which opponents try to build a case. A young leader in a burst of religious enthusiasm may propose: "Let's fast for three days and go out and fundraise!" Someone who hears it, or of it, goes to the media claiming the Moonies are starving people. This is simply not true.

Essentially, our faults concern not evil actions but the mistakes made in trying to accomplish so much so fast. Our visions and dreams have largely become reality. We have moved from a small sect to an institutional church—and we are still growing and evolving. Now, with the many marriage blessings and the children being born, we need to go on to plan for health programs, schools, even a college. We are doing those things. Perhaps some of the bad press and the hostility from clergymen is out of envy. The intensity of our efforts, however, and the utter self-sacrifice of our members, are amazing.

Other criticisms of our church are not really the result of any mistakes on our part. These criticisms arise from the great difference between contemporary American culture and the customs followed in the Unification Church. For example, while the larger culture tends to ignore the significance of age, we show a special respect for elders.

Sometimes we are accused of worshipping Reverend Moon as if he were God. This is patent nonsense. We respect all elders, not just Reverend Moon. He is, however, the founder of our church and, we believe, the example of God's love that we respect most in our world. Criticism of Reverend Moon, I believe, reflects conscious or unconscious racial prejudice. As he said when he was indicted in New York for tax evasion, "I'm on trial because I'm a yellow man and my religion is Unification Church.'' We are not responsible for these negative and morally wrong feelings.

Finally, perhaps the biggest mistake the Unification Church has made in these past dozen years was to not realize how bitter the opposition to our ministry would become. We never foresaw how the government would attempt to discredit our leader. In our ignorance, we failed to see how public opinion sways judges, legislatures, and even government agencies.

When funds were put into a Chase Manhattan Bank account in Reverend Moon's name, it was done for the benefit of the church. After all, the Catholic bishop of a diocese often holds the title to all church accounts and church property. It is part of the function of being a religious leader to hold in trust the funds given by the faithful to spread the Good News. After public hostility arose against him, the IRS brought charges that Reverend Moon held these funds for himself. Nothing could be further from the truth. All of the money, whether brought here or raised by fundraisers from abroad, was used for church purposes. This account goes back to the earliest days when Reverend Moon first came to America, in 1972-1973. At that time members raised money and simply gave it to him for church purposes. It went into the account under his name, but in trust for the whole church. Indeed, the fact that large amounts of money raised in untraceable cash by street fundraisers and from church members from abroad were deposited in this account, and thus put on virtual public display, shows that Reverend Moon never had any intention of defrauding the government.

167

But we forgive those who persecute us. We offer them love, too. If we have sinned against love or against God's purpose or, for that matter, against any law or honest principle, we are ready and committed to correct our sins. Are they who have sinned against us ready to do the same?

10 / Our Vision of the Future

The past dozen years have been a rollercoaster ride—hurried, exuberant, wild, funny, sad, and victorious. In 1972 I joined forces with a tiny group of spiritual seekers and we have been moving forward at breakneck speed ever since. Today I feel my church stands at the threshold of new, exciting possibilities, although we remain under fire from the anti-religious movement, the press, and, more recently, from government agencies and the courts. My hope is that this book and, hopefully, more objective media reporting in the future, will help reduce the prejudice and hostility directed toward us. For, above all, we want to get on with Kingdom-building, and we have much to do. Kingdom-building, however, demands a vision of the future, while we still seem to be engulfed in darkness. James Reston, in a column for *The New York Times* entitled "What's Going On" (March 23, 1983), wrote:

WASHINGTON, March 22 - The Center for Defense Information is a think tank in Washington that keeps a box score on the wars, rebellions, and other violent uprisings going on in the world. Its latest report reminds us of some things we're inclined to forget:
* In the last three years, six new wars have started while only two have ended—with over four million

people engaged in combat.

* Forty-five of the world's 164 nations are involved in these wars, and even the C.D.I. can merely estimate that the number of people killed ranges from one million to five million.

* About 500,000 foreign combat troops are involved. There are ten conflicts in the Middle East/Persian Gulf, ten more in Asia and Africa, seven in Latin America, and three in Europe. Five are conventional wars and 35 are internal guerrilla struggles.

* The United States and the Soviet Union and its satellites are the major suppliers of military arms to 13 nations now at war, and in 1981, the 45 nations involved in 40 conflicts spent over $528 billion on their armed forces.

These, of course, are only rough estimates and cannot take into account the suffering of families or the loss of property, but they remind us of the madness and cost of violence in a world where half the human race is going to bed hungry every night.[1]

Reston's description is similar to the image Matthew Arnold used to describe nineteenth-century Europe: ignorant armies clashing by night. The *Bible* tells us that a nation without a vision must perish; a world without a vision must certainly perish. Reverend Moon is above all a man with a vision of the future, and he is willing to work hard to make his vision a reality. At a

1. James Reston, "What's Going On", Copyright © 1983 by the New York Times Company, reprinted by permission.

time when so many people are opting for the hedonistic pleasures of the moment, Reverend Moon offers a profound vision for a sane and healthy world.

A central component of his vision is the awareness of a loving God as the creator and sustainer of the universe. If God exists, we must understand and proclaim His existence as the center of all life and meaning. A primary task of the Unification movement, then, is to unite all religious people in proclaiming the existence and significance of God. We must, as a united religious people, recognize that there are forces hostile to the idea and the existence of God, and we must analyze, critique, and counter these forces.

If atheistic materialism, Marxism-Leninism or any other type of godless dogma, is to dominate human minds, serious consequences will follow. Millions of people have been killed in nations dominated by Marxist-Leninist thought, not out of some strange aberration in the social fabric, but because of the very nature of a Godless, materialistic ideology. If people are considered merely matter in motion, then it is easy to persuade some that others do not matter much. If we believe that progress must necessarily and inevitably come through conflict, the Marxist-Leninist dialectic, then it is easy to motivate people to violence, war, and terror. Religious people must understand the nature of God if they are to comprehend the infinite value of each individual life. They must understand the purpose and principles through which God works if they are to avoid the Stalinist temptation.

The Unification movement, in its vision of the future, is dedicated to the elimination of all forms of totalitarian control over human life. With God as the center of its value system, the Unification world view celebrates the freedom of the individual who is motivated by a deep respect for human life and culture. We will continue to sponsor programs for professors, students, media, artists, fishermen, and every other profession to emphasize the need for absolute values as the reference point for any activity. In an age that has lost its clear sense of value, we.are committed to a process of value committment in open and free dialogue.

As I travel around the United States I am aware of a profound sickness that afflicts our nation. A series of articles in a Miami newspaper reveal that the drug traffic through that city will approach several billion dollars this year. The San Francisco newspapers report a new epidemic in that city: venereal disease. *The New York Times* runs a front page story on child abuse, while the *Chicago Tribune* presents a look at children of divorced parents. To repeat these themes risks losing impact, for readers have become numb to what appears to be a litany of what is all too familiar.

Rather than acquiesce in silence to the sea of troubles around us, we in the Unification movement seek to take up arms against them. We seek to revitalize the nuclear family as the atomic unit by which to bring new stability and health to the larger community. We wish to be models of mature, God-centered human beings who are public-minded and public-spirited. We seek to raise our children to be ethical people of character, virtue, and nobility, who are committed to the well-being of human civilization.

I looked at my small daughter this morning playing

with my mother-in-law, who is seventy-four years old. I see my mother-in-law filled with joy as she cares for her, and I see my daughter secure in the knowledge that she is loved deeply by her grandmother. My daughter and sons see the respect we give to their grandmother, and they are learning the respect and love they must give to all older people if our civilization is to survive. Grandparents, parents, and children living in harmony at, for us in the Unification movement, a model for the larger world. It is a vision of peace that looks backward as well as forward.

Reverend Moon is very much a part of our vision of the future, for he is an example to us of a human being who is filled with moral passion in a world that is neither hot nor cold. He has taught us that the truly worthwhile life is one dedicated to the highest ideals, and that it is our responsibility as human beings to exhibit the fullness of our reason, the abundance of our creativity, and the depth of our love. "Life may be problematical," he would often say, "but we are problem-solvers. God has given us a great framework of value by which to solve problems. We must, however, make great effort, using great creativity, knowledge, and values to solve our problems."

His life is written large for most of us to see. Some are frightened that one man could seek to do so much for so many, and they are troubled. They are frightened and troubled ultimately, I believe, because they themselves are confronted with what they are and what they could be. Hans Kung, the theologian, has written that the Christian challenge is to become fully human. The human challenge, Reverend Moon believes, is to exercise fully our divine nature, especially our divine love. That is the heart of his vision of the future.

The problems that involve technology, international debt, even volunteerism are all ones that Reverend Moon sees as part of our future. However, he believes that none can be dealt with adequately unless we clarify the nature of the healthy self and the healthy society. He is asking us to approach the future by going back to basics: What is the nature of our being? What is the best way to establish peace on earth, good will toward all human beings?

When the pilgrims came to this new land aboard the *Mayflower*, they came with a vision of the future. It was a vision of a new Jerusalem, a land of peace and freedom where they could live in love. Aboard the *Mayflower* they signed a compact pledging themselves to renew their covenant with God by establishing a community of love among themselves. They knew that if they failed to fulfill their pledge, then surely God's wrath would break out against them.

Those pilgrims were not naive fools. They had experienced the corruption of religion and politics in Europe, but believed they could redeem the false with a new start. James Burns, in his prize-winning book *The Vineyard of Liberty*, points out that the American Revolution was a moral as well as political revolution. The American tradition, going back to the pilgrims, was at its heart a tradition of moral vision. The first generation to come of age, spiritually, after the revolution, were the transcendentalists: Emerson, Thoreau, Whitman. They, too, saw the infinite possibilities of a democratic people guided by spiritual and moral vision.

Even today, Americans are stirred when presidents like John F. Kennedy or Ronald Reagan speak about this nation being guided by a Divine Providence.

Unfortunately, Americans have not yet lived up to their vision. Indians were brutally and wantonly killed, while black men, women, and children were enslaved. Today, our nation still suffers from religious bigotry and racism. To bigotry, no sanction!

In my sixteen years of college teaching I trust that I imparted substantial knowledge to my students, but the thing I could not really give them was hope in a significant vision. I feel that my present work is an extension of a long journey that began with a walk to a synagogue. It is the same walk, and it is the same search for a vision of a loving, creative community. That is really what the Unification movement is all about.

Reverend Moon has said that the purpose of the Unification Church is to wither away. There would be no need for the Unification Church if people were truly living a life of God-centered love, seeking to end the hatred of race against race, nation against nation, people against people. That is the world we are trying to build. It is the age-old vision. It is the vision of God, and it is the vision of every decent human being.

What do we want? We want to feel healthy as human beings. We want to feel that we as individuals can enjoy our bodies and minds, and not feel the pain of guilt, or the confusion of meaningless lives. We want to live in a healthy family, we want to love our children, we want to be honored and respected by men and women. We want to know that our wives and our husbands are faithful, trusting, loyal, and beautiful human beings.

175

We want to live in communities where we are not afraid to walk at night. I like to take walks at three o'clock in the morning. I would like to walk even through Central Park some mornings at three o'clock.

When I arrived in New York City to assume my responsibilities as president of the church, the plane landed at 5:50 a.m. It was still dark, but I went to the Holy Ground in Central Park and prayed that I could do something for this city. I had a vision of New York as a great, big heart that had been badly hurt, violated, ruptured. I felt at that moment that my mission here was to heal that heart.

I have never met anybody who did not want peace on earth, goodwill to all human beings. For us in the Unification movement, however, peace and goodwill is not just a question of sending a Christmas card once a year. We believe in the living Christ, and that each of us can imitate Christ. When Reverend Moon was asked, "Are you the Messiah?" he said, "Look, you be the Messiah, I'll be the Messiah, let the man next to me be the Messiah, let's all work to be the Messiah. Let's all take seriously the messianic calling, for God is looking for someone to respond to His vision. . . . We want to be the sons and daughters of God by sharing God's suffering, by sharing His desire, by sharing His hope, by sharing His will, and by sharing His love."

By the fruit they shall know him. Reverend Moon is a good human being. We Unificationists must show that fact by our actions. I want our church in the future to be known by what we do, more than by what we say. I want to make the world envious of our actions, and in that way let people realize that we are the hope of the future. This is the basic vision that we can give to the world. It is a classic vision, but it is one that must be given to every generation. Every generation feels the impulse of hope. Every generation so far has had that impulse crushed. However, we understand the meaning of the fall of man; it represents a loss of hope, a falling away of trust, a falling away from innocence. What we want to do is to recreate innocence in a world of experience. We want to embrace the world as it is, not to curse it, but to bless it. That is our hope for the future. We want to bring forth light from where there is darkness, to work rather than sit still lamenting the fate of the world. That is our great task, our great mission, and our great challenge as a church here in America, and as a movement, as a people throughout the world. For, after all, when all the churches are forgotten, there is only one human family, if we can make it a family.

FOOTNOTES
"TO BIGOTRY NO SANCTION"

Chapter II

1. James W. Fowler, From an adaptation of *Life Maps: Conversations on the Journey of Faith* by Jim Fowler and Sam Keen, edited by Jerome Berryman, copyright © 1978 by Word Inc. as used in *Stages of Faith* by Jim Fowler (Harper & Row, 1981), used by permission of Word Books, Publisher, Waco, Texas 76796.

Chapter IV

1. Duk Moon Aum, "From Schoolmate to Disciple," *Today's World,* June 1982, p. 6.
2. Won Pil Kim, *Father's Course and Our Life of Faith* (London: HSA-UWC Publications, 1982), pp. 49, 62.
3. Won Pil Kim, "From Pyongyang to Pusan," *Today's World*, April 1982, p. 12.
4. Won Pil Kim, "Father's Early Ministry in Pusan," *Today's World*, May 1982, p. 12.
5. *Ibid.*, p. 15.
6. Gil Ja Sa Eu, "My Testimony," photocopied essay in Unification Theological Seminary Library, Barrytown, New York, p. 27.
7. "God's Hope for America" in *New Hope: Christianity in Crisis* (New York: HSA-UWC Publications, 1974), p. 61.

Chapter V

1. Reverend Sun Myung Moon, *The Way of Tradition*, Vol. 4 (New York: HSA-UWC Publications, 1980), p. 175.

2. Reverend Sun Myung Moon, *Divine Principle*, fifth edition (New York: HSA-UWC Publications, 1977), p. 42.

3. Reverend Sun Myung Moon, *The Way of Tradition*, Vol. 2 (New York: HSA-UWC Publications, 1980), p. 2.

Chapter VI

1. It was originally founded under the name the World Relief Friendship Foundation.

2. Kem Mylar, "Serving the Needy," *Today's World*, July 1983, p. 27.

3. Kehaulani Haydon, "IRFF/ECOPROF hailed as Zaire's 'salvation,' " *Unification News*, December 1983, p. 9.

4. Ronald Johnson, "Harlem takes to farming," *Unification News*, December 1983, p. 17.

5. Frederick Sontag and M. Darrol Bryant, et al., *God: The Contemporary Discussion* (New York: Rose of Sharon Press, 1982), p. v.

Chapter VII

1. Helen Jackson, *Convent Cruelties* (Toledo, Ohio: self-published, 1919).

2. Bamber Gasciogne, *The Christians* (London: Johnathan Cape Ltd., 1977), p. 26.

3. (New York: T. Mason & G. Love).

4. *Ibid.*, p. 8.

5. Flo Conway and Jim Siegelman, *Snapping: America's Epidemic of Sudden Personality Change* (New York: J. B. Lippincott Company, 1978), p. 225.

6. Lee Coleman, *Psychiatry and the Faithbreaker* (Sacramento, California: Printing Dynamics, 1982), p. 8.

7. Margaret Singer, "Coming out of the Cults" reprinted from Psychology Today Magazine, Copyright © January 1979 (American Psychological Association).

8. 14 December 1978.

9. 11 March 1977.

10. 2 November 1978.

11. 8 May 1980.

12. *Los Angeles Herald Examiner*, 18 November 1979.

13. Harvey X. Cox, "Myths Sanctioning Religious Persecution"; *A Time for Consideration*, eds. M. Darrol Bryant and Herbert Richardson (New York: The Edwin Mellen Press, 1978), pp. 3-19.

Chapter VIII

1. "*Playboy* Interview with Ted Patrick," March 1979, pp. 53, 58, 77, 120, Copyright © 1979 by *Playboy*.

2. Ted Patrick and Tom Dulack, *Let Our Children Go* (New York: E. P. Dutton Company, 1976), p. 96.

3. *Ibid.*, p. 18.

4. William F. Willoughby, "Now—Deprogramming for Everyone", *Washington Star*, 18 December, 1976, p. D8.

Chapter X

1. James Reston "What's Going On," Copyright © 1983 by The New York Times Company, reprinted by permission.